Karl Shaw now manages a graphic design studio for an advertising agency. He lives with his wife in Stoke-on-Trent, Staffordshire, and is the author of *The World Encyclopedia of Lies and Utter Fibs*.

GROSS

A Compendium of the Unspeakable,
Unpalatable, Unjust
and Appalling

Karl Shaw

Virgin

First published in Great Britain in 1993 by
Virgin Books
an imprint of Virgin Publishing Ltd
332 Ladbroke Grove
London W10 5AH

ISBN 0 86369 791 7

A catalogue record for this title is available from the
British Library

Typeset by TW Typesetting, Plymouth, Devon
Printed and bound in Great Britain by
Cox & Wyman Ltd, Reading, Berks

CONTENTS

WHAT'S THE WORST JOB YOU EVER HAD?

When Catherine the Great found out that she was suffering from dandruff she had her hairdresser locked in an iron cage for three years to prevent him from telling anyone else about it.

Because many Japanese Sumo wrestlers (average weight about 320lb) are literally too fat to wipe their own backsides, novice wrestlers are expected to do it for them. Apparently six out of every ten novices run away from work in the first year of apprenticeship.

Patent screw manufacturers Nettlefold & Chamberlain, the firm behind British Prime Minister Neville Chamberlain's personal fortune, pioneered an unorthodox approach to health and safety regulations in the 1930s. None of the company's dangerous factory machinery was fitted with safety guards, and serious injuries occurred often. Noting that the cries of wounded workers tended to distract other employees from their jobs the management slapped a big fine on anyone who screamed when injured.

The ancient Egyptians were martyrs to their bowels: believing that all diseases were diet-related, they binged on laxatives and purged themselves for three days at a time. The court official who supplied the enema to the Pharaoh was given the title Shepherd to the Royal Anus.

If you can't stand the heat . . .
In 1671 the French royal chef Vatel realised that it was just going to be one of those days when the roast beef ran short at Louis XIV's banquet and only two cartloads of fish turned up instead of the twelve he had ordered. Rather than face a lot of awkward and embarrassing questions from the king, he committed suicide by running onto his own sword.

Marie Curie's epic work exposed her to such massive amounts of radium that even the notebooks she used are dangerously radioactive to this day. She worked for years on thousands of pounds of radioactive waste in an outdoor shed with no protection from the lethal fumes. Mme Curie expired in 1934 from a particularly horrible form of leukaemia.

In 1901 a Chinese government official sent out to deal with tax-dodgers in the province of Kwan-si was boiled and eaten by the locals.

The executioner John Thrift was a convicted murderer who was set free on condition that he did the government's dirty work as an axeman. Thrift wasn't the ideal candidate for the job on account of the fact that he couldn't stand the sight of blood. When he was called upon to execute the Jacobite rebel Lord Balmerino at the Tower of London in 1745, he fainted, then lay on the ground sobbing while onlookers tried to persuade him to get on with it. When Thrift finally took up his axe, he took five blows to sever Lord Balmerino's head. The public never forgave his ineptitude. When he died a jeering mob pelted his coffin and his pall-bearers with stones and the rotting bodies of dead cats.

In the court of Imperial China, human wet nurses were trained to suckle the royal Pekinese puppies.

Jack Black was Queen Victoria's longest serving Royal Rat and Mole Destroyer. Although he was nearly killed three times by rats and once found that a rat had bitten clean through a bone in his finger, snapping it in two, Black didn't mind because he got to eat as many rats as he could take home with him. Rats, he said, were 'moist as rabbits and twice as nice'.

A taste of religion

The unluckiest missionary of all time was Father Jean de Brébeuf, who was at the receiving end of the worst ever recorded torture session. The Jesuit priest was part of an expedition to Canada in 1649 when he and his fellow missionaries fell foul of a particularly bad tempered band of Iroquois Indians. Brébeuf tried to convert his captors to Christianity, who reciprocated by chopping his hands off and then stabbing him all over his body with various iron instruments. Red-hot tomahawks were suspended around his neck, while a belt made of bark and smeared with pitch was tied around his torso and set alight. The tortures were carefully designed to guarantee a slow, agonising death, yet the still-conscious priest continued to annoy his captors throughout with a non-stop flow of preaching. They seized burning sticks from a fire and stuck them down his throat, but when even this didn't silence him they cut off his lips and soaked him with boiling water. Then they cut chunks of flesh from his legs, arms and torso, roasted them in a fire and ate them while he watched. Before death finally came, they amputated his feet then scalped him for good measure.

At the turn of the century American manufacturers of X-ray equipment were keen to demonstrate their exciting new machinery in department stores and public places. In 1896 the enterprising X-ray machine salesman Herbert Hawks set himself up in a busy shopping precinct and focused rays on his head so that passers-by could see his jawbone on a screen. He stopped doing it after a few days when he lost his hair, eyebrows and eyelashes, his eyesight deteriorated, his gums bled, his fingernails stopped growing and the skin peeled off his chest.

When the tenth Sultan of the Ottoman dynasty Sulaiman the Magnificent was injured in the field, his body was taken to a tent where his doctor struggled valiantly in the midst of battle to save his life. When the Sultan eventually died, his followers were so desperate to keep it a secret that they strangled the doctor to avoid a leak before the Sultan's son Selim could be told.

A perk of the job . . .

Monks in the Middle Ages were usually given the job of keeping vigil over the dead bodies of the wealthy and high-ranking. The custom was stopped after several cases of monks raping dead women were reported.

Workers at the Royal Mint used to be supplied with free drinking vessels made from the skulls of executed criminals spiked on Tower Bridge. They were told that ale drank from the skulls was a great cure for respiratory ailments caused by working in a metal foundry.

Courting the muse

The Turkish historian Abdi drew the short straw when he was selected to write a running biography of Mahomet IV, one of the more demented Ottoman Sultans. One evening, when Mahomet asked Abdi what he had written about his reign that day, Abdi tactlessly replied that he hadn't written anything, as nothing of any interest had happened. Without hesitation the Sultan impaled him with a hunting spear, and said, 'Now thou has something to write about.'

Hard day at the orifice

Ancient Egyptian embalmers weren't popular at parties, mostly because they usually stank of rotting human flesh, but also because word had got around that embalmers had been caught raping female corpses. Families of female corpses, especially beautiful female corpses, often delayed sending their loved ones to the Necropolis for embalming until they had been dead for several days to discourage rape by the embalmers. The mummification process, which in all took about 70 days, began with the removal of the corpse's brain, usually through the nasal canal with the aid of long brass needles with hooks on the end, or occasionally by removing an eye and breaking through the upper wall of the eye socket.

The US Radium Corporation, which made a fortune in the 1920s from producing millions of luminously painted watch dials, fish bait and dolls' eyes, found itself at the centre of a national scandal in 1924 when dozens of their female painters, some only twelve years old, began to fall ill and die horribly and mysteriously. An independent enquiry into the deaths learned that in order to produce the fine artwork needed on the watch dials, the girls were expected to lick excess luminous paint from their brushes: some of the girls even painted their teeth and lips for a lark. The company meanwhile consistently denied that there was any link between the deaths and the tiny amounts of radioactive material used in the paint. Then in 1925 the company chemist Edwin Lehman, although never directly in regular contact with the deadly paint, also suddenly fell dead. The autopsy found that Lehman's bones were so radioactive that, when left on an unexposed photographic plate, they photographed themselves.

In 1971 a Californian involved in a minor traffic accident confessed to the arresting patrolman that he had recently eaten a social worker. He wasn't hungry, he was just trying to make a point.

To humour the Japanese Emperor Hirohito's food-poisoning phobia, every scrap of his food had to be first laboratory tested by scientists for signs of contamination, then served on sterilised plates. Even the royal faeces and urine had to be chemically analysed afterwards. His chef Tadoa Tanak committed ritual suicide when his master died. The Japanese royal ritual of food-tasting before every meal wasn't banned until 1989.

Banquets in the Imperial court of the Chinese Emperor Shih Hu, who ruled between AD 334 and 349, were a trying time for the girls in his harem, and not particularly good news for his guests either. He would select a girl from his harem, have her beheaded, then cooked and served to his visitors. Shih Hu tried to impress by passing the uncooked head around on a platter for his guests to inspect before they ate it so he could show them that he hadn't sacrificed his ugliest mistress.

Sorry . . .

In January 1895 a dispute over trading rights resulted in an attack by more than 1,000 angry tribesmen, led by King Koko, on the British-owned Niger Company on the Niger Delta in Akassa. The native chiefs later sent a letter to Britain addressed to the Prince of Wales, apologising profusely for having taken the law into their own hands, and in particular for eating his employees.

In 1993 a Peking man beat to death a six-year-old schoolboy and left his severed head on a bus. Thirty-six-year-old Ge Yunbao explained that he was irritated at having been passed over for promotion.

Going through the motions . . .

A very select band of palaentologists specialise in the study of excrement, ancient and modern. They can pinpoint a stool's exact age and anal origin by its texture, shape and the tiny barrel-shaped eggs of the parasitic worms that dwell within it. This exclusive club has a membership of only 15 to 20 experts worldwide. They correspond regularly, occasionally meet to swap notes and probably have their own handshake.

YOU ARE WHAT YOU EAT

The Chinese are still the world's biggest dog lovers, especially when they are fried, minced or stewed or served with chilli. Although it is now illegal to eat them, dogs in China are still divided into three traditional categories – hunting dogs, watch dogs and edible dogs. Two great favourites today are dog dumplings and braised dog in brown sauce.

One hundred and seventy-eight tons of tomato ketchup are eaten daily.

The only animal excluded from the SAS Survival Manual as a potential meal, even in the most dire of circumstances, is the common rat.

In parts of Asia fresh ape brain is still regarded as a delicacy and an aphrodisiac. The animal is killed immediately before the meal and the brains are eaten raw.

Rat meat sausages are considered a delicacy in the Philippines.

Been there, eaten that . . .

The eccentric 19th-century geologist William Buckland, famed in 1875 for the discovery of dinosaur dung in Lyme Regis until his find was denounced as a fraud by the Royal Geographical Society, devoted his spare time to travelling the world indulging in offbeat gastronomic experiences. Buckland dined on crocodile, hedgehog, mole, roast joint of bear and puppy. Although he was prepared to eat anything that moved, he admitted that he wasn't too wild about horse, and said the foulest thing he ever ate was stewed mole and bluebottle. Buckland's greatest claim was to have eaten the heart of Louis XIV, which had been plundered from his grave during the French revolution and had found its way into the possession of Buckland's friend the Archbishop of York. For the long suffering Mrs Buckland there were even more trying times ahead: their son Francis not only inherited, but pushed to new limits his father's indiscriminate eating habits. After experimenting on his fellow students at Oxford by serving them mice on toast, Buckland Jnr went on to form the Society for the Acclimatisation of Animals in the United Kingdom, ostensibly to teach the British public how they could ease food shortages by eating new types of meat, but it was mainly an excuse for Buckland and his mates to munch their way through boiled and fried slices of porpoise head, boiled elephant's trunk, rhinoceros pie, grilled panther, garden snails, slug soup and earwigs. At a Society formal dinner in 1862 Francis and his friends enjoyed a blowout of Japanese trepang sea slug, steamed and boiled kangaroo, wild boar, roasted parrot and leporine.

When Prince Charles and Princess Diana visited Korea in 1992 they were fed roast dog, but it could have been worse. Koreans have such a high regard for Spam that there is even a black market for it.

At a state dinner during the Queen's visit to Belize in 1985 she was fed roasted rodent. Royal-watchers noted that the Queen appeared to 'pick' at her food.

When Nicolae Ceaucescu visited the Queen at Buckingham Palace in 1978 he took his official food taster with him to make sure he wasn't being poisoned.

British vivisectionists now perform ten times more experiments on animals to test environmentally friendly or 'green' consumer products than they do to test cosmetics.

In 1985 a building worker in Bangkok died after eating his favourite lunch-time snack, four bags of locusts. An inquest recorded that it was the DDT in the locusts, not the locusts themselves, that had killed him.

If thine pie offend thee . . .
A unique case of food contamination happened in October 1992, when nine people complained that Linda McCartney's brand of vegetarian pies had been spiked with steak and kidney. Linda said she was 'horrified'.

In Paris in 1594 during a siege by Henry of Navarre, starving townsfolk fed themselves by making bread from the ground bones collected from the crypt of the Holy Innocents.

The average Briton eats about 9lb of chemical food additives every year.

Hitler and Mussolini both had syphilis. Churchill didn't, but his father Randolph did.

The Frenchman Noël Carriou killed both of his wives because they were poor cooks. 54-year-old Carriou was sentenced to eight years in jail in 1978 after killing his second wife for cooking him an overdone roast. Seventeen years earlier he broke his first wife's neck after she served him an undercooked meal. In passing sentence the judge sympathised with Carriou: good cooking, he said, was an important part of married life.

Darling, you've got coffin on your breath . . .
A 42-year-old Frenchman Michel Lotito, who works by the stage name Monsieur Mangetout, has a unique digestive system which enables him to make a living from eating metal, wood, glass and anything else that tickles his fancy. His diet to date has included ten bicycles, several supermarket trolleys, 80ft of steel chain, TV sets and a whole Cessna light aircraft. Monsieur Mangetout has also eaten a brass handled 6ft 6in by 3ft

coffin: according to *The Guinness Book of Records* this is the only known case of a coffin ending up inside a person.

In March 1992 an American bread company was taken to court after a woman in Los Angeles found a used condom in a large loaf.

Although only about ten per cent of the cases will be reported, over 650,000 Britons will have suffered food poisoning this year. If food contamination continues to increase at the present rate, by the end of the 1990s the annual figure will be around one million.

The frogs' legs eaten as a traditional French delicacy are bullfrogs from the Indian sub-continent. The legs are the only valuable part of the frog, so they were traditionally ripped off while the still-living discarded torso was left to crawl away. This practice was banned in 1985, and the frogs are now killed by electric shock.

The world's most exclusive coffee is made from a bean which has already passed through the colon of a civet cat.

In the late 1980s while approximately one third of the world's population was underfed, the EEC destroyed 2.5 million tonnes of vegetables and fruit per annum to maintain prices.

Good old Victorian values

Although it is widely held that modern-day food is relatively less 'natural' than it used to be, meal-times in Queen Victoria's day were a far more risky and often lethal activity because business morals in the catering industry were never lower. Deliberate food adulteration, with no effective laws to stop it and the incentive of a quick profit, grew to horrific proportions as food suppliers cheerfully ripped off and poisoned their customers at the same time. The most common well-organised frauds included the use of ground Derbyshire stone instead of flour, fake Gloucester cheese coloured with red lead, baked horse offal from the knacker's yard in coffee, lead chromate in mustard and even iron bars baked in loaves to make weight. People died after eating green blanc-mange coloured with copper sulphate and yellow Bath buns which owed their coloration to arsenic. Fifteen people died after buying sweets from a Bradford market which were found to be laced with white arsenic. Beer drinking was possibly the most dangerous pastime of all: over 100 convictions were obtained in one year for contaminating beer with dangerously poisonous substances, including sulphuric acid which was added to 'harden' new beer, and iron sulphate, added to give it a good frothy head.

Paté de foie gras is produced exclusively from the livers of force-fed geese. Some geese have their feet nailed to boards while they are forced to eat 5.5lb of salted fatty maize a day.

In 1992 the London Natural History Museum re-issued a Victorian booklet called 'Why Not Eat Insects?', which included tempting recipes for slug soup, curried lice, fried wasp grub caterpillars and moths on toast. Entomologists point out that by the middle of the next century food shortages will force us all to change our attitudes to what we eat anyway, so we may as well get used to the idea of popping out for a Big Mac cockroachburger.

The Japanese eat dolphins' testicles as a highly prized delicacy.

Before every major Spanish bullfight there is a pre-fight 'bulls' testicles on toast' party.

The ancient sailors of Spain and Portugal regularly ate dead rat on long voyages. During Magellan's ill-fated attempt to circumnavigate the world, his crew sold rats to each other for one ducat each.

White veal, originally introduced to Britain from Holland, requires the cruellest form of factory farming. Within a few days of its birth the calf is taken from its mother and put into a small crate, and for fourteen weeks denied fibrous food and force-fed solely on liquid milk substitute. The calf is deliberately starved of iron so that the meat stays white.

When Sir Walter Raleigh brought tobacco and potatoes back with him from the New World they got a mixed reception. Spuds were immediately branded a health

*hazard because they caused syphilis, scrofula, flatulence
and unnatural carnal lust. Tobacco, on the other hand,
was thought to be completely harmless.*

The Guinness Book of Records now refuses to publish
unusual gastronomic records, acknowledging that such
feats are not only very dangerous but also in dubious
taste, but that hasn't stopped some people from trying.
Records held include the eating of cooked dog (3.5lb of
dog meat in 18 minutes 10 seconds), baked beans (4lb
13oz in 10 minutes), eels (2lb in 32 seconds), cockroaches
(28 in 4 minutes), earthworms (60 in 3 minutes 6
seconds), raw eggs (13 in 1.4 seconds), live maggots (100
in 5 minutes 29 seconds) and slugs (12 in 2 minutes).

One of the most persistent arguments in favour of
vegetarianism was that a meatless diet bred peace-lov-
ing, gentle people – until World War II, that is. Both
Hitler and Mussolini were vegetarians.

At least 20 per cent and as much as 80 per cent of the
chicken sold daily in the UK is already infected with
salmonella.

LOONY DICTATORS

When Idi Amin became ruler of Uganda the occasion passed by without a murmur of dissent from the international community, who believed him to be semi-literate, stupid and arrogant, but harmless. It didn't dawn on them that Amin was also dangerously insane until he volunteered to marry Princess Anne.

Haiti's President 'Papa Doc' Duvalier was an expert in violence and intimidation, but his speciality was fraudulent election fixes. When his countrymen went to the polls in 1961 they found pre-printed at the top of each ballot sheet the words 'Docteur François Duvalier, President'. When the votes were counted it was announced that Papa Doc had been unanimously re-elected because, after all, his name appeared on every ballot paper. A few years later he used a familiar tactic to prolong his stay in office *ad infinitum*: when Haitian voters were asked, 'Do you want your President elected for life?', the answer was a convenient and resounding 'yes': sadly, there wasn't room on the ballot sheet for a 'no' box.

Francisco Lopez, President of Paraguay from 1862–70, was not only the craziest, but also the ugliest and the most obese of all South America's dictators: one of the more flattering descriptions of him was 'a tidal wave of human flesh'. Lopez had a Napoleonic fixation (he kept one hand tucked inside his jacket at all times) and a fearsome Irish wife named Eliza Lynch, who helped influence much of his career. He spent most of his reign waging a hopeless war against Paraguay's neighbouring enemies Argentina, Brazil and Uruguay, and trained his men so hard that many didn't live long enough to see a battle. This, combined with Lopez's refusal to allow any of his men to surrender, reduced the male population of Paraguay by nine-tenths. Once, in an attempt to deceive the Brazilian army at the battle of Acosta Nu, he sent out a battalion of small boys wearing false beards. Lopez's incompetence meant that the military situation grew ever worse, so he organised a spying system which encouraged every third man in his army to spy on his comrades, and to shoot anyone, including officers, who showed any sign of cowardice. The resulting widespread paranoia among the ranks led to many of his men marching into battle backwards because they feared their own side more than the enemy.

To mark the anniversary of his military coup in 1977, Idi Amin invited the former Prime Minister Edward Heath to fly to Uganda 'with his band' to play before him during the celebrations. Amin said he regretted that Mr Heath had been demoted to the obscure rank of bandleader, but noted that he'd heard that Mr Heath was one of the best bandleaders in Britain, and offered to assist the ex-PM with a supply of goats and chickens. By now the British were used to Amin's philanthropic gestures: he once offered to send a shipload of vegetables to England to solve the recession.

The North Korean leader Kim Il Sung compelled the entire population of his country to wear lapel badges with his face on them.

Jean Bokassa, 'Emperor' of the former French colony the Central African Republic was another dictator with a Napoleonic fixation. Although his country was officially rated one of the poorest in the world he blew £10 million – about one third of his country's annual budget – on a bizarre 48-hour coronation binge to celebrate his 'promotion' from President to Emperor in 1977. Although all of the world's top political leaders were asked to attend, most including Britain and the USA contemptuously returned Bokassa's invitations. Many foreign dignitaries, including ambassadors from Italy and West Germany did however turn up to the imperial banquet held in the capital, Bangui. What they didn't know was that Bokassa had arranged to have twelve selected inmates from Bangui prison butchered and served to his dinner guests.

Idi Amin once refused to attend the Commonwealth Games unless the Queen sent him a new pair of size-13 boots.

In 1986 the electors of San Mateo county, California, voted in Brendan Maguire as sheriff with an overwhelming 81,679 majority. It was only after the results were announced that someone pointed out that he had already been dead for two years.

When 'Papa Doc' Duvalier discovered that tourism in his country was down by 70 per cent, he was torn between his need for revenue and his natural mistrust of foreign troublemakers. He decided on a compromise. He launched a publicity drive to tempt the visitors back, then had the corpse of a dissident flown into the capital Port-au-Prince, where it was left to rot in public: it was strategically placed by an exit from the airport next to a sign which read 'Welcome to Haiti'.

In 1980 Imelda Marcos had a 'mystical vision' which prompted her to blow $100 million on a bizarre attempt to create a Philippino version of the Cannes film festival. Most of the money was spent on an extravagant new film theatre. The builders and everyone else associated with the Marcos family were so corrupt that no one was particularly surprised when in 1982, two months before the official opening, half of the building collapsed killing at least thirty workers. To avoid delaying construction she had concrete poured over the dead men and had the theatre exorcised to appease the superstitious. The grand opening went ahead almost exactly as Imelda had planned, with just one minor setback: she had invited the Pope, but in the event had to settle for Brooke Shields. Imelda's second International Film Festival in 1983 was even more farcical: in order to recoup the huge losses incurred by her first effort she showed pornographic movies.

Before he became President of Haiti 'Papa Doc' Duvalier spent two years in hiding from the government of the day dressed as a woman, and at meal times habitually switched dinner plates with his 'friends' to avoid being poisoned.

Over 500 people died building Louis XIV's monumental folly the Palace of Versailles, mostly from fevers and epidemics caused by the insanitary conditions his workers were expected to live and work in and numerous fatal building site accidents. Louis was slightly embarrassed by the death toll and banned his courtiers from discussing it.

When things started to go badly for Paraguay's mad President Francisco Lopez he organised a mass suicide pact and ordered the entire population of his nation's capital Ascuncion to march off into the jungle with him. Lopez changed his mind at the last minute and ordered the national treasure to be thrown off a cliff into a deep jungle instead. The treasure was swiftly followed over the cliff edge by all of the witnesses to ensure secrecy.

Dinner guests at Idi Amin's State House in Entebbe were treated to some unscheduled entertainment by their host in August 1972. Between courses, Amin suddenly vanished into the kitchen and returned with the frozen head of his former commander-in-chief, Brigadier Hussein. Amin screamed abuse at the head and threw cutlery at it, before asking his guests to leave.

'Papa Doc' Duvalier claimed he could predict the future from late night conversations he had with a severed human head, which he kept in a cupboard in the presidential palace. It belonged to one of his former army officers Blucher Philogenes, who had led a doomed CIA-backed invasion of Haiti in 1963.

The lack of good boots has been the perennial problem of marching armies down the centuries. In World War II German soldiers on the Russian front found their boots were far less capable of keeping their feet dry through the freezing winter than those of their Soviet opponents, so the resourceful Germans found a practical way to strip the frozen dead soldiers of their footwear. They collected frozen bodies and sawed their legs off at the knee. Legs and boots were then placed in an oven until they were sufficiently thawed out for the boots to be removed.

Ex-Ethiopian leader Colonel Mengistu Haile Miriam kept an unusual keepsake under the floorboards of his office. This was where police found the remains of the former Emperor Haile Selassie in 1992.

One of Idi Amin's two favourite hobbies was erecting statues all over Uganda to his greatest idols, Queen Victoria and Adolf Hitler. The other was crushing the genitals of his victims with his bare hands.

In addition to the 1,200 pairs of shoes that the Philippine government confiscated from Imelda Marcos, they also swiped her only bulletproof bra.

Mussolini originally adopted the Roman style straight-arm greeting as the fascist salute because he thought that shaking hands with people was unhygienic.

Idi Amin was a former heavyweight boxing champion of Uganda. When his country was being overrun by Tanzanian troops in 1978, he suggested that he and Julius Nyerere settle the war between them in the ring with Mohammed Ali as referee.

In 1870 the Paraguayan President Francisco Lopez declared himself a Saint of the Christian Church. When the matter was put to the bishops of Paraguay, the twenty-three who did not agree were shot. 'Saint' Francisco was duly anointed and that date officially entered into the Christian calendar. His final act was to have a new medal minted which he awarded to the entire population of Paraguay, or at least what was left of it.

'Emperor' of the former Central African Republic Jean Bokassa had 200 ragged schoolchildren beaten to death in the 1970s by his Imperial Guard. Their crime was failure to comply with school uniform regulations.

Idi Amin handed out a mass murder contract to his private police force, the implausibly named State Research Bureau. The SRB simply rounded up candidates and murdered them, then informed the families that for £150 they would lead them to the body. The scheme became such a huge success that neighbours complained about the ceaseless din of machine gun fire at SRB headquarters. To keep the noise down, Amin bribed his prisoners to execute themselves by clubbing each other to death with 16lb sledgehammers. Amin's favourite place for disposing of his enemies was Lake Victoria: it was said that when the lights went out in Kampala, everyone knew that the hydro-electric generators on the Lake's Owen Falls Dam were once again clogged with human bodies. The scale of Amin's campaign of terror against his enemies was so immense it was bound to run into logistical problems. A former government employee Francis Kalimazo recalled that he was at a wedding when he learned of his own 'death' on the radio. He then realised that he was part of the backlog.

'Papa Doc' Duvalier had the Lord's Prayer rewritten for use in Haitian schools: 'Our Doc, who art in the National Palace for life, hallowed be Thy name by present and future generations. Thy will be done in Port-au-Prince as it is in the provinces. Give us this day our new Haiti, and forgive not the trespasses of those anti-patriots who daily spit upon our country . . .'

When the Ethiopian head of state Colonel Mengistu Haile Miriam unleashed his 'red terror' against so-called counter-revolutionaries in 1977, he picked on mostly children and young students and had many hundreds massacred. He allowed parents to buy the bodies back for burial. He called it 'paying for the bullet'.

A British diplomat who proposed an easy way of assassinating Hitler with a sniper's bullet had his plan turned down by the British government because it was 'unsportsmanlike'. General Sir Noel McFarlane was military attaché at the British Embassy in Berlin in 1938 when his plan was turned down by Whitehall. He calculated that the shooting could be easily done during one of Hitler's frequent public appearances.

In 1978 Idi Amin planned a full scale invasion of neighbouring Tanzania, but first decided to lull Tanzania's President Julius Nyerere into a false sense of security. He sent Nyerere a telegram which read, 'I love you so much that if you were a woman I would consider marrying you.'

Kim Il Sung had every road in North Korea built with an extra lane for his sole private use.

When 'Papa Doc' Duvalier needed advice on matters of state he mostly got it by sitting in his bathtub wearing a black top hat while consulting the entrails of a dead goat.

Nicolae Ceaucescu and his wife Elena had a phobia about germs. On one occasion they planned to go on a 'walk-about' for publicity purposes, which required them to shake a few hands and kiss small children. The secret police selected a few volunteers beforehand, had them locked up for weeks and regularly disinfected in readiness for the big day.

Idi Amin was incensed when his former wife Kay was found dead in her apartment after a clumsy abortion attempt. He took her 6-year-old son and Amin's newest and youngest wife, Sarah to visit her in the mortuary. When they arrived they found that her head was back to front, her legs had been sewn onto her shoulders and her arms attached to her pelvis. Amin solemnly explained, 'This what happens to bad women.'

Francisco Lopez had his 70-year-old mother publicly flogged and executed because she confessed to him that he was a bastard.

As well as being the world's most influential shoe buyer, in the late 1970s Imelda Marcos became the world's single biggest buyer of jewellery. She had stores open at night for private showings, while her bodyguards paid for her gems with thousand-dollar bills stashed in paper bags. As she always insisted on a discount, shop owners always put their prices up by 25 per cent as soon as they knew she was coming, then offered her fifteen per cent off.

The Shah of Persia, Nasir Ud-din, became well known to the British public in Victorian times for his visits to Buckingham Palace, and his enormous moustaches. He once visited an English prison, and when he was shown the gallows, asked if he could see someone being hanged. When he was politely told that this wouldn't be possible, as no one was about to be executed, the Shah pointed to his entourage and said, 'Take one of my suite.'

Speculation the about mental state of Libya's Colonel Muammar Gadaffi has been rife for years: Egypt's late President Anwar Sadat was so worried by Gadaffi's behaviour that he tried to persuade him to have a brain scan. The CIA are in no doubt at all that Gadaffi is completely barking mad, and have a lengthy dossier of detailed files on his movements to prove it. A 1985 report states that he made a trip to Majorca wearing make-up and carrying a teddy bear.

When Saddam Hussein's war with Iran was going badly and morale was low, he called a meeting of his cabinet ministers and told them he was considering resignation. Most took the hint and insisted that he stay on. His health minister alone took him up on the offer and agreed that Saddam should step down. Saddam coolly took him into the next room, shot him in the head, and sent the man's butchered remains home to his wife in a shopping bag.

MANNERS MAKETH MAN

When the Earl of Oxford, Edward de Vere accidentally broke wind while bowing to Queen Elizabeth I, he was so embarrassed by the incident he decided to keep a low profile, and threw himself into extensive travelling abroad. When he finally returned to the court after a seven year absence, the Queen greeted him with, 'My Lord, I had forgot the fart.'

The famous German physician Carl Ludwig wrote a pamphlet explaining why so many ladies in the 19th century suffered from chronic constipation. Women, he explained, had a fear of accidentally farting after eating, and suffered from too much tensing of the buttocks. He called it 'the green sickness'.

The Old Testament book Ecclesiasticus recommends clearing the stomach by throwing up before or during a big meal to make room for more food.

Fijian cannibals usually ate with their hands, but as a mark of respect for the dead used a ritual wooden fork for eating people.

The Romans were prolific meal-time vomiters finding that it was an effective way of preventing a hangover the next day. They even evolved a special technique to encourage it – they tickled their gullets with peacock feathers. The Emperor Claudius I tried it, and choked to death in the process.

In some Latin and Mediterranean countries, loud public belching is a sign of appreciation after a good meal.

During the feast of Ramadan, Moslems are not allowed to swallow even their own saliva.

Found in the lost property department of the Scotland to Midlands rail line in 1947: three artificial limbs, a glass eye, a two-headed carp and a three-legged chicken.

Aristophanes, Chaucer, Rabelais, Swift, Ben Franklin and Mark Twain have all written about farting. Erasmus once wrote a treatise about flatulence and belching, and warned that a stifled fart was a health hazard.

Nineteenth-century English gentlemen had 'smoking chairs' designed with secret drawers under the seat in which a chap could spit.

The ancient Greeks made elaborate bronze pans for vomiting and urinating in at meal times.

Claudius I was so troubled by the notion that thousands of Romans were risking their health by stifling farts he passed a law permitting people to break wind freely in company.

The British soldiers who went over the top at the Battle of the Somme on 1 July 1916 were told that, after heavy bombardment of enemy positions, the only Germans they would meet would be dead ones. Some officers advanced armed only with swagger sticks or umbrellas, while others kicked footballs towards the German lines and charged after them.

We piss anywhere, man

When the Shah of Persia arrived at Buckingham Palace in 1873 for a brief stay with Queen Victoria, it was noted that he repeatedly failed to use the royal lavatories and went wherever the spirit moved him.

Casanova was offended by the sight of Londoners dropping their pants and urinating openly in busy streets. He suggested that the very least they could do was face the street so that their backsides were not exposed to passers-by.

Rock and roll's most celebrated three pints of urine, released against a garage wall on 18 March 1965, helped cast the Rolling Stones as Britain's Public Enemy No. 1. The notorious leak took place at a service station in Stratford, east London, after a garage attendant refused them admission to the toilets. Mick Jagger explained, 'We piss anywhere, man.' Jagger, Bill Wyman and Brian

Jones, described in court as 'shaggy haired monsters', were charged with insulting behaviour and fined £5 each.

The legendary bank robbers Bonnie and Clyde were eating bacon and tomato sandwiches when they were ambushed by a posse of patrolmen, led by a Texas Ranger, and perforated by 77 bullets, splattering bits of brain all over the car upholstery. Local souvenir hunters scoured the car for trophies, even cutting off locks of Bonnie Parker's hair. One was stopped by a coroner as he tried to saw off Clyde Barrow's ear.

When nature called the Spanish First Division footballer David Billabone during a game between his club Bilbao and Cadiz, he decided he couldn't make it to half-time and discreetly urinated behind a goalpost. Unfortunately he wasn't discreet enough to escape the attention of a 20,000 crowd and a local photographer, who splashed a picture of the leaking Spaniard all over Spanish newspapers. Billabone was fined £2,000.

The crowned heads of Europe held their breath when Peter the Great became the first Russian czar to travel west in 1697. Peter was noted by nearly everyone he met to have been incredibly dirty and smelly, even by 17th-century standards, and blissfully unaware of rudimentary personal hygiene, table manners or even basic potty training. For the duration of the czar's visit to England he and his friends were accommodated in a mansion belonging to Sir John Evelyn. Sir John later presented a bill for £350 to the British government for damage to his property, which included vomit and excrement smeared on the walls and floors.

For centuries the Church actively discouraged priests from eating beans in case they broke wind during solemn holy rituals.

Till breath do us part . . .
According to ancient Jewish law, bad breath is sufficient grounds for divorce.

KEEPING IT IN THE FAMILY

Pills made from the toxic metal antimony, highly esteemed in mediaeval times as great bowel regulators, were handed down from father to son and from mother to daughter as precious family heirlooms. The pill irritated the intestinal tract, causing loose motions, and would pass through the body unharmed.

After the execution of Sir Walter Raleigh in 1618, his head became the Raleigh family heirloom. His widow Elizabeth kept it for 29 years before passing it on to their son Carew, who looked after it until 1666 when it went with him to his grave.

The 18th-century Chinese Emperor Qianlong planned to bring the whole of Europe to its knees by banning rhubarb exports, thereby creating a constipation epidemic.

The famous duellist Brian Maguire, a descendant of the ancient Fermanagh family and an officer in the East India Company, couldn't bear the thought of life without his son George when the boy died aged twelve in 1830. Maguire decided to craft a permanent and cherished keepsake: he embalmed the boy himself and kept him

in a glass case which he carried with him everywhere –
until his own death five years later of a heart attack.

Ancient Egyptians didn't always bury their dead relatives after their bodies had been mummified. Families
often observed the grisly ritual of keeping the body at
home with them so that it could be symbolically present
at meal times, and some were kept above ground for
several years. There was another reason for this practice: at the risk of ruining appetites and frightening the
children the mummified bodies of dead relatives were
valuable assets which could be used to guarantee loans:
i.e. you could borrow money on the surety of your stiff
mother, father, brother or child. Anyone who failed to
discharge a debt would be refused a burial of their own.

The family that slays together, stays together
An infamous experiment in the 'Good Life' was practised
by Britain's grossest ever family in 15th-century Scotland. At the head of the family was the demented
Sawney (Sandy) Beane, born in East Lothian, a few
miles from Edinburgh. The young Sawney and his new
bride ran away to make themselves a home in a cave
on a deserted part of Galloway on the wild, west coast
of Scotland. There, they incestually increased the Beane
clan to 8 sons, 6 daughters, 18 grandsons and 14
grand-daughters. The result was a family who made the
Addams, the Munsters, and even the Windsors look well
balanced. The Beanes progressed from stealing sheep,
to preying on passing travellers – probably hundreds –
and took to cannibalism as the best way of filling their
stomachs and getting rid of the evidence. The family
became so notorious that in 1435 James I personally led

a 400-strong posse to try to flush them out. They quickly found several members of the family red-handed, attacking a man and murdering his wife, and the trail soon led them to the Beane lair with its well-stocked larder of corpses, mostly dried, pickled or salted. The adult members of the family were eventually put to death following a show trial at Leith. The men had their hands, feet and sexual organs cut off and were left to bleed to death: the women were forced to watch, then burned alive.

When he took office in AD 37 Gaius Caesar, better known by his nickname Caligula, or 'little boots', was at the age of 25 already considered to be monstrously demented even by Roman Emperor standards. As a 13-year-old he had an incestuous relationship with his sister Drusilla, and spent most of his evenings stalking the streets with his guards, indulging in wild orgies with prostitutes, then burning their brothels down. At the age of 26 however he fell ill with a fever, and when he recovered he was even more deranged than usual. He ordered his three sisters Drusilla, Agrippinilla and Lesbia to leave their husbands to share his bed. When Drusilla became pregnant he became convinced that the child was his own and was endowed with God-like powers. He couldn't wait for the birth and had Drusilla disembowelled and the unborn baby cut from her womb.

The most generous last wills and testaments of all were left by endo-cannibals, i.e. cannibals who eat and are eaten by members of their own family. A dying

Ecuadoran Indian would often leave a will, detailing which of his body parts were to be left to which lucky relative. Once the will had been read, the funeral became a major culinary event. The dead relative's corpse was roasted, cut into pieces and consumed by grieving relatives. The head was generally kept until it was ripe with maggots, then the brains were spiced and eaten.

After Thomas More's head was hacked off, parboiled and stuck on a pole on London Bridge in 1535, his daughter Margaret bribed a bridgekeeper to let her steal it and take it home – a crime for which she was later arrested and briefly imprisoned. The head was buried with her when she died in 1544.

Where there's a will . . .

The wife of an eccentric London dentist Martin van Butchell (1735–1812) decided to repay her husband for years of marital misery with a spiteful will which decreed that her fortune pass to a distant relative 'the moment I am dead and buried'. Her resourceful husband quickly found a loophole in the will by keeping her body well above ground. Van Butchell, a skilled embalmer, fitted her out with a new pair of glass eyes, and filled her veins with oil of turpentine and camphorated spirit of wine. She was then dressed, propped up in the drawing room and put on public display from 9 a.m. to 1 p.m., from Monday to Saturday. The rush to see the corpse was so great that van Butchell was forced to restrict viewings to private appointments only. When he remarried, his new wife took an instant dislike to the ex-Mrs van Butchell and ordered her out of the house. The corpse was presented to the Royal College of

Surgeons, where it remained for more than 150 years until the museum was destroyed by Hitler's bombers.

Circumcision probably began as a harvest ritual. Some ancient peoples believed that the penis contained magical life-giving properties, and regularly planted cut-off foreskins in their fields to produce better crops.

When the poet Percy Bysshe Shelley drowned in 1822 he was cremated, but as an afterthought his friends saved his heart from the flames and presented it to his wife Mary. She kept it with her, wrapped in silk, everywhere she went for the rest of her life. When their son Percy died the poet's heart was buried with him.

Hannah Beswick of Cheetwood Hall, Lancashire lived with a constant fear of being buried alive. When she eventually expired in 1758 aged 77, she left £25,000 to her doctor with instructions that he regularly inspect her corpse for signs of life. Her body was embalmed and crammed inside a grandfather clock with a velvet curtain tastefully draped across the glass viewing panel. One hundred and ten years after her demise the trustees of her estate agreed that Hannah Beswick's state of health was finally beyond dispute, and she was granted a decent burial.

The Canaanites were one of several communities along the eastern Mediterranean who worshipped, and made offerings to dung, to ensure regular evacuation of the bowels.

By the time Eva Peron died of cancer in 1952 an eminent pathologist had been on stand-by for a fortnight to embalm her. With Eva barely dead he quickly filled her veins with alcohol, then glycerine, which kept her organs intact and made her skin appear almost translucent. Her funeral turned into a riot: as two million Argentinians filed past her coffin, seven people were crushed to death. Eva's husband Juan planned to have her housed in a giant mausoleum, but he was forced to suddenly flee the country, and the body went missing for several years. In 1971 however Juan and Eva were touchingly re-united. According to an eye-witness, Eva's corpse was ever-present at the Peron family dinner table along with Juan and his new wife Isabel.

Faeces are a girl's best friend . . .
In 1992 the Tokyo Metropolitan Sewerage Bureau advertised personal 'jewellery' made from recycled human waste. They acknowledged that the product known as 'sludge jewellery' isn't quite the same as the real thing, but it's the thought that counts.

MAD . . .

In an attempt to make himself more attractive to his girlfriend Gala, Salvador Dali shaved his own armpits until they bled and wore a perfume made of fish glue and cow dung.

The Duke of Wellington had more to occupy his mind at Waterloo than the small matter of defeating Napoleon. Wellington's ally, the famous Prussian field marshall Leberecht von Blücher, suffered from fits of senile melancholia which led him to experience bizarre hallucinations. Blücher once confided to Wellington that he was pregnant and about to give birth to an elephant, and that moreover the cad who had raped him was a French soldier.

Although the press baron Lord Northcliffe went completely mad in his later years, his editors were still obliged to follow his instructions because he was still the boss. Northcliffe once cabled the editor of the *Daily Mail* complaining that there weren't enough giraffes in the Teddy Tail comic strip, and on another occasion instructed him to publish the entire contents of every menu on board the ocean liner *Aquitania*. Northcliffe later became convinced that the Germans were trying to assassinate him by poisoning his ice-cream. He once cabled George V: 'I am turning Roman Catholic.' The King cabled back: 'I cannot help it.'

The deranged Emperor Nero had crucified Christians covered in tar and set alight to form avenues of glowing human torches to show spectators the way to Christians versus Lions contests.

The German poet and dramatist Friedrich von Schiller couldn't work without placing his feet on a block of ice and inhaling the fumes of rotting apples.

Behind the battlements of their Grand Seraglio Palace, the Ottoman Sultans of Turkey perfected a traditional method of assassination. It involved strangulation with silk bowstrings, performed by deaf mutes who had their eardrums perforated and their tongues cut out to make them candidates for the job. The practice began with Mahomet the Conqueror (1431–81) who introduced a law which stated that his successors had the right to execute their own brothers to help smooth the path of succession and avoid unnecessary sibling rivalry. When Mahomet III took the throne in 1595, his father's dedicated work in the harem meant that the new Sultan had to murder his nineteen brothers all aged under eleven, and throw seven of Murad III's pregnant mistresses into the river Bosphurus. Thereafter, close male relatives were spared execution and instead incarcerated in a windowless cell called 'The Cage' with only deaf mutes and sterilized concubines for company, sometimes for as long as 50 years. By the time the new Sultans came to power they were more often than not completely insane. The practice was finally abolished in 1789, but by then hereditary madness was already firmly established in the Ottoman line of succession.

There are 92,000 Americans currently on a waiting list to go to the moon.

The poet Virgil spent the equivalent of £50,000 on the funeral of his pet fly.

The wealthy 19th-century naturalist and explorer Charles Waterton was noted for anti-social behaviour which earned him affectionate respect as one of England's great eccentrics, whereas similar behaviour by a less affluent person would have earned a one-way ticket to Bedlam. Waterton loved to exhibit his prized collection of stuffed animals around his home, but found orthodox taxidermy too boring. He kept himself amused by grafting parts of different animals onto each other, and once surprised his dinner guests by displaying the partially dissected corpse of a gorilla on his dining table.

Michelangelo was severely psychopathic and showed signs of schizophrenia.

Although Edgar Allan Poe never actually spent time in an asylum, he was said to have been certifiably insane. Poe was an alcoholic and laudanum addict but it didn't stop him joining the local Temperance Society and giving lectures on the evils of drink. In 1849 he was found lying in the gutter suffering from *delerium tremens* and died a few days later.

The American artist James Whistler once dyed a rice pudding green so that it wouldn't clash with the walls of his dining room.

The mad Russian Czar Paul became obsessed with the idea that his soldiers should look great, even at the expense of military efficiency. He made them wear uniforms that were so tight fitting that breathing was difficult and fighting impossible. Under their uniforms they wore straitjackets to make them stand erect, and on their heads thick, heavy wigs with iron rods inserted in them to make them sit straight. To prevent his soldiers' legs from bending when they marched he had steel plates strapped to their knees.

Peter the Great tried to pay for his almost perpetual warmaking by imposing massive taxes on beards and beekeeping.

The transvestite King Henri III was the most bizarre of a very long line of very odd French royal sovereigns. The 'King of Sodom', who ruled France from 1574 to 1589, appeared at official ceremonies in full drag and was regularly followed by an entourage of rent boys, known as his *mignons*.

General George Custer was an unstable egomaniac who went on from being the most incompetent student in his class at West Point to become one of the US Army's most incompetent generals. Custer was also a cowardly commander who, by massacring 103 Cheyenne, earned the nickname 'squaw-killer'. Every one of Custer's 211 men were scalped at Little Big Horn – save Custer himself. Perhaps fearing the worst, he had already had his famous golden locks shorn off in favour of a close crew-cut.

In the 1960s the American Society for Indecency to Naked Animals (sic) claimed a membership of 50,000 people who were dedicated to forcing animals to wear clothes for the sake of decency. The Society's president, Clifford Prout, asserted that his pressure group was so strong that within a few years it would be normal to see dogs and cats wearing trousers. In 1963 they picketed the White House in an attempt to make Jackie Kennedy clothe her horse.

*Mr Prout explained that the Society's somewhat mislead-
ing name was due to an unfortunate grammatical error
which could not now be changed for financial reasons.*

The operatic composer Giacomo Mayerbeer lived with a
constant fear of premature burial. He arranged to have
bells tied to his extremities so that any movement in
his coffin would attract attention.

Samuel Johnson was a hypochondriac who often begged
his wife to lock him in his room and shackle his legs
because he was convinced he was going mad.

In Phnom Penh in 1972, two people were killed and fifty
injured when hundreds of Cambodian troops suddenly
opened fire at the moon. *The Times* reported that the
soldiers had fired into the sky to prevent an eclipse of
the moon by a monster frog called Reahou, who wanted
to eat the moon and must be stopped.

... BAD ...

The Mongol conqueror Genghis Khan was not entirely without compassion. He once decided that a defeated foe, who turned out to be a former childhood friend, should be spared the usual bloody and merciless execution. He had him rolled in a carpet and kicked to death instead.

The Ottoman Sultan Mahomet III enjoyed watching women's breasts being scorched off with hot irons.

Between 1935 and 1938 in Cleveland, Ohio, the Mad Butcher of Kingsbury Run slaughtered at least twelve people, mostly vagrants, by chopping the bodies into small pieces then leaving them in piles in alleys and on wasteland. The body parts were often mixed, and few of the heads were ever recovered. The killer was never identified.

The favourite pastime of the Roman Emperor Tiberius was to sodomise young boys. If they protested he had their legs broken.

46

Britain's all-time busiest mass killer was Mary Anne Cotton, born in 1832 in a Durham pit village. Her chosen method of execution was arsenic poisoning. She killed at least 15, and probably up to 21 people, including three husbands, eight of her own children, four step-children and her mother. She died horribly: her bungled hanging on March 1873 took several minutes to complete.

The childhood hobby of the Russian Czar Ivan the Terrible was throwing live dogs off the Kremlin roof 'to observe their pain'.

The Roman Emperor Tiberius became bored with the array of tortures in fashion at the time, and decided to invent a few of his own. His favourite was to force the victim to drink vast quantities of wine until the bladder was at maximum pressure, then tie up his genitalia with a lute string. Tiberius was such a well-respected torturer that many of his prisoners committed suicide as soon as they were accused, rather than bother waiting for the trial.

When Caligula ran out of money he found a novel way of raising cash – he opened his palace as a brothel, and high-ranking members of the Senate were forced to pay 1,000 gold pieces each for the privilege of having sex with his sisters. They were then ordered to send their wives and daughters to work with his sisters in the palace brothel. Caligula was finally killed when one of his guards ran a sword through the Emperor's genitals;

another group of guards meanwhile murdered his wife then dashed out the brains of his baby daughter against a wall.

The insane Mongol leader Tamurlane, a descendant of Genghis Khan, has been described as the most spectacular sadist of all time. When he conquered Sabzawar in 1383 he had 2,000 prisoners built into a living mound, then bricked in. Later that year he had 5,000 men beheaded at Zirih and their heads made into a huge pyramid. In India he massacred 100,000 prisoners, and in 1400 had 4,000 Christians buried alive.

Although the historical 'Count Dracula', Vlad Tepes, had an unparalleled appetite for sadism, he was nevertheless considered a hero in his country. Tepes, who ruled over Walachia (now part of Romania) between 1456 and 1476, had about 20,000 of his enemies impaled on wooden stakes, and enjoyed drinking the blood of his victims. In his spare time he forced wives to eat the roasted bodies of their husbands, and parents to eat the flesh of their own children. He was also a brilliant general and was adored by his fellow countrymen because he defeated their sworn enemies, the Turks. When a large troop of Tartars strayed into his territory, he selected three of them, had them fried, then forced the others to eat them. When Turkish envoys arrived at his palace to sue for peace, he had their hats and coats nailed to their bodies.

Unlike Tiberius, Caligula and Claudius before him, Nero didn't enjoy watching men die because he couldn't stand the sight of spilled blood. He preferred to order his enemies to commit suicide: they usually did.

Napoleon III had his cheeks rouged before the Battle of Sedan in the Franco-Prussian War of 1870, so that his men couldn't see that he was white with fear and ravaged with dysentery.

America's busiest mass murderer was the former New Hampshire medical student Herman Webster Mudgett. During the Chicago Exposition in 1893 he seduced, drugged and murdered young girls in a house on 63rd Street, which was known as his 'Torture Castle'. After murdering his victims Mudgett burned and dissolved the corpses in acid or lime, saving the best bits for further experimentation in his upstairs laboratory. When police searched his home they found the remains of 200 corpses, but there must have been many, many more. He was hanged on 7 May 1896.

During the Holy Inquisition, first unleashed by the Catholic Church in the mid-15th century, a woman could be tried as a witch for simply being old enough, ugly enough, or being in possession of a cat, a wart, or red hair. Some of the ingenious tortures devised by the Dominicans to extract confessions from witches were subtle, some less so. In Germany, suspect witches were force-fed salted herring then denied water. Some had spikes forced beneath their fingernails and toenails and the soles of their feet burnt: others visited the rack, the 'Spanish Boot', or were whipped, scourged, had their limbs dislocated, or their bodies filled with water. Most confessed. Historians have calculated that the total number of victims to have been between five and six million.

The full force of the Holy Inquisition at its most brutal was saved for a religious sect known as the Waldenses, who had settled in the Piedmont region of northern Italy. One of the favourite methods of torture used by the soldiers was to place small bags of gunpowder in the mouths of victims and set fire to them. Records show that one Bartholomew Frasche had holes drilled through his heels and ropes passed through the wounds, and was dragged through the streets. Daniel Rambaut had his fingers and toes amputated a joint at a time until he promised to be a good Catholic. Sara Rastignole had a sickle thrust through her lower abdomen. Martha Constantine was raped and her breasts removed. Mary Pelanchion was stripped naked, and hung head first from a bridge so that soldiers could use her for target practice. Jacopo di Rone had his nails torn off with red-hot pincers and holes bored through his hands, and strips of his flesh were cut off with a sword until he agreed to go to Mass.

Ivan the Terrible ruthlessly exterminated potential

rivals for power including members of his own family, and bashed out his son's brains with a club. He died, however, playing chess.

The Nantes lawyer Jean-Baptiste Carrier was a French Revolutionary in a hurry, for whom the guillotine was far too slow and inefficient. He had his victims packed into barges, towed into the River Loire, then drowned. Couples were stripped naked and tied face to face, while Carrier's henchmen stood on the river banks with axes in case anyone escaped drowning. The water became so polluted with human corpses that fishing was banned. Carrier also discovered that the guillotine was an unsatisfactory method of beheading infants. The heads of tiny children were chopped in half because their necks made too small a target for the blade: one executioner collapsed and died from a heart attack after beheading four little sisters. Instead Carrier had 500 children rounded up in a field then shot and cudgelled to death.

The Sultan Ottoman Osman II enjoyed archery practice on live pageboys.

Mussolini was the first 20th-century dictator to make torture official state policy. His blackshirts invented their own technique – they would pump a prisoner full of castor oil to 'purge him of the will to live'.

In 1975 President Julius Nyerere's Tanzanian police forced confessions from prisoners by inserting hot chilli peppers into their eyes, nostrils, ears, mouths and anuses.

Monty Python's Flying Circus satirised the 1960s London gangland scene with a sketch featuring Doug and Dinsdale Piranha, two brothers who terrorised victims by nailing their heads to the floor and screwing their pelvises to cake-stands. The inspiration for this famous sketch came not from the Kray Twins Ron and Reggie, but from the Richardson gang, who terrorised south London at around the same time. Although the Krays earned more notoriety, in terms of sheer sadism the Richardsons were in a league of their own. Led by Charles Richardson and his younger brother Eddie, they specialised in torture. While Charles dressed up in judge's robes, victims were tried before kangaroo courts, then had their teeth removed with pliers and electrical generators attached to their testicles with crocodile clips. The Richardsons' *tour de force* however was staking victims to the ground with six-inch nails then removing their toes with bolt cutters.

Pol Pot, the Cambodian whose philosophy of Rural Revolution wiped out three million of his fellow countrymen, was a former Buddhist monk.

The Turks evolved a new method of assassination during the reign of the Ottoman Sultans in the 17th century: a cup of Turkish coffee was laced with chopped hair and ground glass, which was guaranteed to destroy the victim's intestines during a long and painful death.

When Ivan the Terrible conquered Withenstein he had the defeated Finnish leader roasted alive on a spit.

Indian tax collectors in the 19th century persuaded defaulters to pay up by forcing them to drink buffalo milk laced with salt until the victim was half-dead with diarrhoea.

The people of Rome finally turned on Nero when he had a male slave castrated, then 'married' and lived with him as man and wife. To escape a flogging, Nero finally slit his own throat.

Frederick the Great regularly opened his veins before a battle to calm his nerves.

The Hungarian Sylvestre Matushka had a unique sexual perversion – he was turned on by watching large-scale human catastrophes. As the odds against him coming across more than a couple in a lifetime were not good, he decided to engineer a few himself. In 12 months he derailed two trains with explosives, killing 22 passengers and injuring 16. He was finally arrested in 1932 while attempting a third derailment, and jailed for life.

Thanks to Argentina's Peronist pro-Nazi sympathisers, Dr Joseph Mengele and other leading Nazis were allowed to live openly under their own names when they fled to Argentina after World War II. Mengele was even listed in the Buenos Aires phone book.

When Winston Churchill was Home Secretary in 1910 he advocated that in the interests of racial purity, mentally incompetent people should be neutered and tramps and vagabonds rounded up and placed in concentration camps.

Josef Stalin, who killed more people in 30 years than Ivan the Terrible and all of the other Russian Czars managed in over 400 years, reasoned his behaviour thus: 'The death of a man is a tragedy: the death of a thousand is a statistic.'

The Emperor Heliogabalus was Rome's most celebrated transsexual. After failing to find a doctor who could perform a sex-change operation he settled for castration and 'married' a hunky slave called Zoticus. He called himself the Empress and took to hanging around brothels so that he could satisfy the customers himself.

Heliogabalus was murdered on the lavatory and his body thrown into the Tiber.

The Milwaukee cannibal Jeffrey Dahmer, who admitted at his trial in February 1992 to killing 17 people, performed crude lobotomies on some of his victims in the hope of creating zombie sex slaves.

One in every 1,000 Americans is a murderer.

. . . AND DANGEROUS TO KNOW

Richard Wagner always composed in a stiflingly hot room perfumed with roses while wearing a silk dressing gown, which belied the fact that he was also a notorious womaniser. Wagner was also touchy about critics: he often invited friends around, treated them to a sneak preview of his work then asked them for a frank opinion. Anyone who didn't offer a glowing review would be threatened with physical violence.

Genghis Khan murdered his own brother in an argument over a fish.

Although the names Burke and Hare are commonly associated with bodysnatching, they never actually robbed graves. In the flourishing market of the 19th century 'resurrection' trade they decided to improve their business turnover by cutting out the middle man (i.e. natural death) and creating a few corpses of their own. Burke, who had served as a medical orderly on the battlefield at Waterloo, gave the English language the word 'burking', meaning 'to kill stealthily', originally for the purpose of selling the victim's body for anatomical research. Together, he and Hare stalked the Edinburgh slumlands in the 1820s and accounted for at least 16 victims. Their preferred method of assassination was suffocation: one lay across the victim's chest while the other held the mouth closed and pinched the nostrils.

When General Alexander Haig was asked for his summary of 1 July 1916, the first day of the Battle of the Somme which saw 57,470 British soldiers either dead or dying by nightfall, most of them killed during the first hour of the attack, he replied: 'The general situation was favourable.'

The Ottoman Sultan Sulaiman I used to cure persistent drunks by pouring molten lead down their throats.

While Robert Maxwell was busy stealing around £500 million from his employees' pension funds, at the same time he was appearing in an expensive video production designed to persuade workers that their money was safe in his hands. It was called 'What's The Catch?'

The ancient Indian killer cult Thuggee (hence the word 'thug') was an exclusive club with a strictly controlled membership. In order to retain it, you were obliged to strangle a minimum of one innocent victim a year.

Sir Arthur 'Bomber' Harris's 1,000-bomber raids on German cities during World War II, designed in his own words, 'to do maximum damage and destruction to populated areas' once made even Churchill blanch. During the area-bombing of Cologne in May 1942 the entire city was so completely devastated by fire that late arrivals couldn't find anything left to bomb: one bomber who complained to his pilot that he couldn't find anywhere left to drop his load was told by his pilot, 'Well start a bloody fire somewhere where it's not burning.'

Vivisection claims the lives of 20 million animals worldwide every year. The National Cancer Institute has to date tested 'cures' on half a million animals, with a success rate of only 0.00001 per cent.

When Genghis Khan died in the middle of a siege, his followers were determined that his death be kept a secret until his son and heir Ogatai was safely in control. Khan's final victims were the bystanders who innocently spotted his funeral procession as it headed for the burial ground: they were all put to the sword.

King Philip of Spain passed the most ambitious death sentence of all time in 1568 when he declared that the entire population of the Netherlands (about three million) were heretics and therefore should be executed. It was a tough nut to crack even for Philip's chief executioner the psychopathic Duke of Alva, hired for his efficiency in wiping out heretics. The Duke did however manage to slaughter 800 people in Holy Week. His chosen method of execution was to seal the mouth of the victim with an iron gag which allowed only the tongue to protrude. The tongue was branded with a hot iron so that it swelled and could not be withdrawn. The victim was then burned alive. At Antwerp he executed 8,000 people in one session.

After an attempted rebellion of his troops, the Roman Emperor Domitian extracted confessions by holding a blazing torch under the prisoners' genitals. Courtiers guilty of even the mildest of criticism were crucified upside down. His inevitable assassination in AD 96 was almost a carbon-copy of Caligula's death – he was stabbed in the genitals.

Although he had sent thousands to their deaths, the French Revolutionary Maximilian Robespierre was very squeamish and couldn't stand the sight of blood. Thanks to Robespierre the guillotine in the Place de la Revolution in Paris was so busy that residents in a nearby street complained that the stench of aristocrats' blood from the street stones was a health hazard and lowered the value of their houses. Robespierre was one of the residents.

In 1980 the Chinese attempted to impregnate female chimpanzees with human sperm to develop a near-human hybrid 'for economic and technical purposes'. Dr Qi Yongxiang in the city of Shenyang said the 'near human ape' would do menial tasks and provide substitutes for human transplant organs. The Chinese authorities said

*that as the creature produced would be classified as
animal, there need be no qualms about killing it.*

While the French Revolutionary Jean-Paul Marat was
inciting mobs to attack the jails of Paris in 1791 to
purge them of counter-revolutionaries, Parisian women
wore severed ears pinned to their skirts as souvenirs.
In six days half the population of Paris's prisons was
slaughtered.

The Turkish Sultan Murad IV liked to exercise his 'royal
prerogative' of taking ten innocent lives a day.

The French 17th-century pirate Jean David Nau – 'Le
Lolonais' to his friends – was probably the most feared
of all pirates. He invented his own technique for tortur-
ing prisoners for pleasure. He had a cord tied around
their heads, which he twisted with a stick until the
victim's eyes shot out: this trick was known as
'woolding'. Lolonais's own demise was an altogether
messier affair. He was captured by Darian Indians, who
slowly tore him limb from limb while he was still
conscious then tossed bits of him into a fire while he
watched.

Christopher Columbus fed his dogs on the bodies of
murdered Indians. Natives who were unable to
deliver him with sufficient gold had their hands hacked
off.

When Genghis Khan stormed a town called Termez on
the Oxos river, all of the inhabitants were slaughtered.

As one old woman was about to be killed, she begged the soldier for mercy in return for a pearl. He asked where it was, and she replied that she had swallowed it. The old woman was promptly disembowelled and several pearls were discovered. When Khan heard about it he ordered his men to open up all the dead and inspect their stomachs.

OF LICE AND MEN

Although the Winter Palace of St Petersburg during the reign of Czar Nicholas I was considered to be one of the biggest and most opulent royal residences in the world, it was perpetually alive with vermin. This was mostly due to the Czar's reluctance to get rid of the herd of cows he always kept on the top floor to ensure a regular supply of milk for his family.

The average number of body lice found on an infested human is around 100. The record number of lice found on a single shirt is 10,000 plus 10,000 eggs.

In 1784 an Austrian doctor sparked off an international race for the world's biggest tapeworm when he found a 24ft specimen inside one of his patients. Paris countered with a tapeworm measuring 120ft and weighing over 2lb, but the day was finally won by a Russian peasant who proudly claimed a 238ft tapeworm for his country. There were plenty of quacks who were quick to exploit this new found public fear of worms. Advertising copywriters selling patent worm powders had a field day with torrid stories about people whose lives were wrecked by tapeworms. Promotional material for a product called 'Exterminator' claimed: 'Mr. Stiles of the Lock and Key of West Smithfield was practically eaten by a worm 8ft long, and might still have been alive if only he had taken the "Exterminator" . . .'

In many of the world's tropical areas virtually the entire population is infested with pinworm.

Apart from Howard Hughes's pathological fear of germs which obliged him to spend the last years of his life clad in Kleenex tissues, he suffered from chronic constipation and once spent 28 hours on the toilet. He also had an obsession about his own urine, which he had sealed in glass jars, numbered, dated and catalogued by his aides.

A salmonella germ can pass through 28 sheets of toilet paper.

Apart from the tanks, helicopters and submarines, Leonardo da Vinci also turned his inventive mind to the latter-day problems of hygiene. When he made his plans for 'Ten New Towns' to 'distribute the masses of humanity' he advocated the use of spiral staircases in all of his houses. This, he explained, was to discourage people from urinating and defecating on the landing.

Britain has an estimated three-quarters of a million bedwetters.

The repeated injections of saliva produced by a hungry body louse produces a slight toxic effect that makes the human host feel depressed, or 'lousy'.

The great unwashed
Louis XIV took only three baths in his lifetime, each of them under protest.

Genghis Khan's Mongol warriors were a superstitious bunch who believed that washing was sacrilege. There was also a more practical reason for the lax approach to their ablutions – the thick crust of dirt which covered their bodies throughout their lives helped them to withstand temperatures as low as −43°F. Khan's men used their lack of hygiene as a weapon of psychological warfare: their enemies could smell the festering Mongol hordes long before they could see them and were often paralysed with fear by the time they arrived.

Samuel Pepys is reputed to have never once had a bath in his lifetime.

Eighteenth-century English nobility, when faced with new-fangled standards of personal hygiene, clung to the belief that washing was decidedly non-U. One prominent lady aristocrat who accepted an invitation to a society dinner sat down to eat with noticeably filthy hands. When someone remarked upon the grubbiness of her fingers, she replied, 'Madam, you should see my feet.'

The eleventh Duke of Norfolk was renowned as one of the richest and the smelliest men in England. In his entire life the 'Dirty Duke' never once voluntarily bathed: when his servants found it impossible to occupy the same room as him they used to get him blind drunk and quickly bathe him before he regained consciousness.

Ludwig van Beethoven never really mastered personal hygiene either: his friends had to take away his dirty clothes and wash them while he slept.

The miser John Overs, who made his million by operating a ferry across the Thames from Southwark to the City, lived so frugally that the rats in his house left of their own accord. His meanness led to his death. In an attempt to cut down on his bills, Overs pretended to be dead for a day, believing that his house servants would fast until after the funeral and thus reduce his food bill. The plan backfired when his servants celebrated instead by throwing open the doors to the pantry. When Overs rose from his death bed to complain they thought he was a ghost and clubbed him to death with an oar.

Although the famous waters of Bath in the 17th and 18th centuries were famed for their health-restoring qualities, they almost certainly killed more people than they cured. The waters were hardly ever cleaned or emptied, and the healthy and the sick, the diseased and the unspeakably dirty were able to frolic in, and drink, a vast soup comprising mostly floating ulcers, sweat, dirt and dandruff.

Of the 75 species of bedbug, only two feed on humans. A bedbug can live in your bed for up to four years and can go for eighteen months without a meal.

Stiff Upper Lip

Until recently all British state-maintained establishments had hard toilet paper with the words 'Government Property' stamped on it. Only in the very highest echelons of the Civil Service would you find soft paper.

The first soft toilet tissue, Andrex, was originally developed from a design for gentlemen's paper handkerchiefs and was sold exclusively at Harrods. It wasn't a big hit until Hollywood gossip columnists revealed that the biggest film stars of the day were insisting that their studios obtain Andrex.

A typical household pillow is home to about 2,000 house dust mites, which in turn excrete about 20 pellets of faeces a day. It is estimated that a six-year-old pillow will have approximately one-tenth of its weight comprising old human skin, dead and living mites and mite dung.

In the late 1960s NASA scientists were moved to overcome a new personal hygiene crisis – how to defecate in space with the inconvenience of zero gravity. They came up trumps with the 'space nappy' – one soiled by Alan Shepherd is now in the British Museum. Modern astronauts now use vacuum toilets which suck away the waste as it leaves the body: liquids evaporate, and solids are freeze dried, sealed in bags and returned to earth.

During the Black Death the most popular way of keeping down the stench in houses was to keep a goat in your house: the odour of the goat overpowered the stench of death. Goatless families preferred to wear vinegar soaked rags over their nostrils.

The common housefly transmits 30 different diseases harmful to human beings.

The Djoukous tribe of central Sudan strangled their kings after a rule of seven years before removing the royal brain, heart and kidneys for his successor to eat. In the Niger Delta it was customary for the local ruler to mark his accession to power by entering the palace through a newly-cut door, stepping over the blood of a sacrificed couple, then retiring into his inner sanctum to make a meal of his predecessor's heart.

There are about 10,000 bacteria in every litre of town air, and 100,000 bacteria in one litre of drinking water.

The amputation of the right hand is seen in the Middle East as the ultimate social stigma, mostly because Muslims never eat with their left hand: they use it exclusively to wipe their backsides.

Body lice are highly sensitive to changes in temperature – they will vacate anyone with a fever and quickly leave a dead person. It is said that when the slain body of Thomas Beckett lay in Westminster Abbey, a column of lice evacuated the corpse like a retreating army.

The average amount of faeces defecated by a human during a 70-year lifespan is 2.6 tons.

To help keep pace with the royal bowels of Louis XIV, which were regularly purged with suppositories from infancy (he had more than 400 enemas and purges in the last year of his life), the Palace of Versailles had 264 toilets. They were mostly painted black to signify 'courtly distress'.

The world's most valuable human faeces is a nine-incher known as the Lloyds Bank Turd. The unique Viking stool – so-called because it was found in an archaeological dig under a Lloyds bank – is highly valued because of its near-perfect condition (unusual in a 1,000-year-old turd) and is insured for £20,000.

When George III found a marauding louse on his plate during dinner in 1787 he commanded his entire kitchen staff to have their heads shaved.

GENTLEMEN, JUSTICE
HAS BEEN DONE

Henry VIII invented a new method of execution for
Richard Rosse, cook to the Bishop of Rochester, who had
poisoned the soup at a formal banquet and killed
seventeen people over dinner. The king had him boiled
to death in one of his own stockpots.

The authorised method of execution during the reign of
the Roman Emperor Tiberius was strangulation. There
was however also a law which forbade the strangling of
virgins, but the resourceful Tiberius found a loophole:
he ordered that virgins should first be defiled by the
executioner.

James Scott, the Duke of Monmouth and first-born
illegitimate son of Charles II, was victim of Tower Hill's
messiest execution on 15 July 1685. The handsome and
popular Duke complained loudly that the axeman's
blade appeared to be rather blunt, but no one took much
notice. In the event it was the fifth blow which finally
severed his head from his shoulders just before he had
a chance to say 'I told you so'. The crowd were so
appalled that the axeman narrowly escaped a lynching.
It was belatedly decided that the Duke, being a rather

historically important person, should have his portrait painted for posterity. His head was duly sewn back on, the joins covered up, and his portrait taken. He now hangs in the National Portrait Gallery.

The most prolonged execution in French history was in the pre-guillotine days of 1626, when the Comte de Chalais was publicly beheaded with a sword. His head was hacked off only after the 29th stroke: he was still alive at the 20th.

When California's notorious San Quentin gas chamber was installed in the 1930s it was tested on live pigs. The city authorities were so proud of their 'humane' new system that, in a desperately miscalculated exercise in public relations, they invited newspaper reporters to witness their first disposal of a human being. The reporters were appalled by what they saw: one described it as 'more savage than being hanged, drawn and quartered'.

The chief executioners of Constantinople during the reign of the Ottomans excelled in diverse methods of execution – one of the preferred methods involved drowning by slow degrees. Souflikar, chief executioner during the reign of Mahomet IV, personally strangled 5,000 people over a five-year period.

The USA shares a distinction with Iran and Iraq as being one of only three states to execute the insane and the mentally ill.

When King Henry IV of France was assassinated in 1610, his murderer was tortured with boiling oil and molten lead, then tied to four horses and torn apart.

Wandsworth Prison still has an operational scaffold, which is oiled and tested every six months. It is faithfully maintained to execute people found guilty under the Armed Forces Act of 1971, which still has a nominal death sentence for piracy with violence, treason and other mutinous offences.

Although the Gospels' description of Christ's death is the most famous account of crucifixion, it was a commonplace method of execution widely used throughout the Middle East. As if the lingering death by suffocation on the cross wasn't enough, it was usually augmented by whatever torture took the executioner's – or the mob's – fancy, including broken legs, stoning or flaying the victim's skin. The Romans in particular liked to amuse themselves by nailing the victim up in different positions: upside down was a big favourite.

In 1740 a seventeen-year-old rapist named William Duel was hanged, and emerged from a deep coma to find that his body had been donated to science and a surgeon's knife was busily slicing into his vitals. Duel survived and his death sentence was subsequently commuted to transportation for life.

The frying game
America's most horribly bungled execution by electric chair was also one of the first. In 1893 William Taylor

was condemned for killing a fellow inmate in Auburn Prison. As the first electric charge surged through his body, his legs went into spasm and tore the chair apart by his ankle strappings. The charge was switched off while hasty repairs were made to the chair. The switch was thrown again, but this time there was no current because the generator had burned out. Taylor was taken out of the chair and drugged in an attempt to deaden any pain he may have felt. By the time the power had been restored Taylor was already dead. The law however had to be carried out, so the dead man was once more strapped to the chair and the current was passed through him for another 30 seconds. A warden announced, 'Gentlemen, justice has been done.'

The American murderer James Bullen was sent to the electric chair in Sing Sing in 1932. He recovered on the way to the cemetery, leaped out of the coffin and ran off. They caught him and electrocuted him again.

When Albert Fish was sent to the electric chair in Sing Sing prison in 1936, the first electric charge failed, allegedly short-circuited by dozens of needles the old man had inserted in his own body. Doctors discovered a total of 29 needles in his genitals.

It took three surges of 1,900 volts of electricity, each over a period of fourteen minutes, to finish off John Evans in Alabama state prison in 1983. Witnesses saw Evans struggling for breath as smoke began to pour from the electrodes on his head and one of his legs. The autopsy on Evans's body revealed that he had endured fourth- and second-degree burns while still alive.

Although there hasn't been a public execution in the United States since 1937, the gassing of Robert Alton Harris in 1992 was the next best thing. Harris was puzzled to find that 48 people, including eighteen journalists and a film crew, were allowed in to see California's first execution for 25 years. Several broadcasting companies expressed an interest in screening the gassing.

The guillotine held a morbid fascination for the French medical profession, who marvelled at the speed of execution and speculated on whether or not the brain would continue to function after decapitation. Some people believed that the razor-sharp blade struck the victim so cleanly that they had lost their heads before they knew anything about it, a theory fuelled by dozens of stories about victims who continued to protest after they had lost their heads. Eye-witnesses recorded that when the head of Jean Paul Marat's assassin Charlotte Corday was held up and slapped by the executioner, it showed unmistakable signs of anger. Subsequently French doctors were allowed to carry out various macabre experiments on severed heads, including pinching the cheeks, sticking things up the nostrils, holding lighted candles near to the eyeballs, and even shouting the victim's name very loudly in his ear. In 1880 the murderer Menesclou had the blood of a living dog pumped into his head. It was recorded that the head responded with a look of 'shocked amazement'. Much more recent research by Russian doctors actually gives some substance to these stories: they have found that if for any reason the brain is suddenly cut off from its oxygen supply, it uses an emergency system which effectively manages to keep the victim conscious for several minutes.

In 1992 tenants of an apartment block in a strict Ortho-dox Jewish area near Tel Aviv, Israel, stood by and watched as a fire gutted their homes. They later explained that they had delayed phoning the fire brigade for half an hour while they went to see their rabbi and ask him if it was OK to use a telephone on the Sabbath.

The state of Louisiana abandoned electric chair execu-tions in 1991 because of the pain inflicted on the victim by burns, preferring to execute their criminals by lethal injection on a surgical trolley. In 1992 the legislature was pressed to allow the state to medicate insane criminals so that they can experience the terror of facing death by execution.

Britain's last official executioner Albert Pierrepoint terminated the lives of 450 murderers and traitors during his 25-year career, but he wasn't altogether happy in his work. After resigning he wrote: 'I do not now believe that any one of the hundreds of executions I have carried out has in any way acted as a deterrent against future murder. Capital punishment, in my view, achieved nothing except revenge.'

On average, a new death sentence is passed in America every day of the working week.

Are you sure this thing is safe?

In the 18th century, 'hanging' in Britain consisted of being slowly strangled at the end of a rope. The hangman often had to speed the process up by hanging on to the victim's legs. Recoveries from execution by hanging were not infrequent. The hangman William Marwood made the system slightly less offensive in 1871 when he perfected the long drop, by which the victim fell from six to ten feet thus dramatically reducing the suffering endured by those hanged. The drop caused fracture dislocation of the neck's vertebrae, severing the spinal cord and medulla, and so causing instant death.

Two men have survived three hangings apiece. The murderer Joseph Samuels was reprieved in 1803 after the rope broke twice on the first and second attempts, and the trapdoor failed to open on the third. A trapdoor mechanism also saved the life of convicted murderer John Lee in 1884. Even though it worked every time it was tested, it failed to open three times in the space of seven minutes. Lee was let off with life imprisonment.

A woman freshly hanged in 1724 in Musselburgh, Scotland became the centre of a grisly dispute between her family and a bunch of enthusiastic anatomists. Her relatives were determined to give her a decent Christian burial: a party of medical students meanwhile had other plans for the corpse and were equally determined to get their hands on it. A bloody fight broke out over the body, which settled the argument by suddenly sitting upright. She lived on for another 30 years with a new nickname – 'Half Hangit Maggie Dickson'.

The final words of Dr William Palmer, facing execution on the gallows in 1855 after he poisoned to death fourteen people, were 'Are you sure this thing is safe?'

Since the United States resumed executions in 1977 they have been putting people to death at an average rate of fifteen a year. Texas coined the term 'assembly line executions': they kill more people, and faster, than any other state, and at any one time has 350 people on Death Row.

The guillotine is still the official method of execution in the Congo. The last execution by guillotine in France took place in 1977.

In eighteenth-century London criminals condemned to the gallows were traditionally allowed to stop off at the Church of St Giles-in-the-Field for a last pint on their way to execution. One man, a teetotaller, refused the offer of a drink because he wanted to press on and get it over with, thereby missing a reprieve which arrived two minutes after he was hanged.

In 1752 in London a nineteen-year-old traitor sat up on the dissecting table only minutes after his execution. A quick thinking surgeon responded by clubbing him to death with a mallet.

The Roman emperor Constantine employed an alternative to the most common death sentence of the day, crucifixion: he had molten lead poured down the throats of the accused.

When animal experiments first became widespread at the turn of the century, many of the tests involved reflected more on the mental state of the surgeons than the results they expected to achieve. In 1908 the American Charles Guthrie transplanted the head of a dog on to the body of another dog. The animal survived for a day. In 1950 the Moscow surgeon Vladimir Demichov created a two-headed dog from one large and one much larger animal. The creature lived for 29 days.

China has the world's most refined and most revolting systems for the disposal of criminals, including strangulation, decollation and the infamous Ling-chy, or 'Death by the Thousand Cuts'. The precise technique of Ling-chy varied from region to region, but by and large a basic routine was observed: the executioner was presented with a basket covered with a cloth. Inside the basket was a collection of knives, each knife inscribed with the name of a body part. The executioner selected a knife at random, and proceeded to cut off the listed body part. Desperate relatives of the condemned man would often bribe the executioner to find the knife labelled 'heart' as quickly as possible.

In April 1992, 34-year-old American rubbish-van driver Billy White was executed by lethal injection in Huntsville prison. It took medical attendants 40 minutes to locate a vein and another nine minutes for him to die.

The official method of execution in the Arab states of Saudi Arabia, Yemen, Qatar and the United Arab Emirates is decapitation by the sword.

In America, blacks convicted of murdering whites are eleven times more likely than white defendants to receive the death penalty.

Before he was finally executed in Florida in 1988, William Darden survived six death warrants on last-minute appeals.

English executioners did a roaring trade in selling portions of their victims as souvenirs. The most saleable mementoes were severed hands, which were turned into candlestick holders.

London Bridge became the prime site for displaying the severed heads of executed villains because it was the only route into the city from the south, and served as an early reminder to visitors that they were expected to behave themselves. The heads were first 'parboiled', an embalming technique which involved boiling the head in a large kettle containing salt and cumin seed – the latter used to keep hungry seabirds at bay. It was reported that the head of John Fisher, executed by Henry VIII for refusing to acknowledge his ascendancy over the Pope as head of the English Church, actually got better-looking after it was parboiled and spiked on the Bridge. An eye-witness commented that 'in his lifetime he never looked so well'. The rejuvenated head caused such a stir that after a fortnight the executioner was ordered to take it down and throw it into the River Thames.

The average number of murders in New York State always goes up in the month following an execution.

Albert Pierrepoint's fee for executing Ruth Ellis, the last woman to be hanged in Britain, was fifteen guineas – £15.75p.

TRUST ME, I'M A DOCTOR

Crocodile dung, pigs' teeth, asses' hooves, frog sperm, eunuch fat, fly specks, dried vipers, oil of ants, oil of wolves, earthworms, spiders, human excrement, sweat, semen, hair, the saliva of a fasting man, nail clippings, the sexual organs of various animals, feathers, fur, raw silk, spiders' webs, cast-off snakeskins, jaw bones from the skulls of executed criminals, moss from the skull of a victim of violent death: all of these substances have been used by doctors for treating illness.

Britain's worst ever doctor was Muhammed Saeed, the bogus Bradford GP who was granted a licence after arriving from Pakistan and allowed to work for the National Health Service for 30 years before he was finally rumbled. 'Dr' Saeed was jailed for five years in 1992 after variously prescribing to his 3,000 patients shampoo to be taken internally, creosote for a tooth complaint, sleeping pills to be taken three times a day, cough mixture to be rubbed into the skin, and suppositories to be taken orally.

A drastic remedy for a headache, 'trepanation', was

devised by Stone Age man in the belief that head pain was caused by evil spirits lurking inside the cranium. The prehistoric equivalent of aspirin required at least five surgeons to administer it: four to hold down the patient while the fifth slowly drilled a hole through the patient's head with a sharpened flint. The evil spirits could then escape through the hole, thus relieving any discomfort. Some skulls were trepanned more than once: the record is held by an Inca migraine sufferer whose skull was perforated seven times.

A highly effective method of tooth extraction was practised by Dr Monsey, Resident Physician to the Chelsea Royal Hospital, home of the Chelsea Pensioners. He took a strong piece of catgut, wound one end around the patient's tooth then threaded the other end through a specially prepared bullet with a hole drilled through it. The bullet was loaded into his revolver and fired.

The ancient Greeks thought that toothache was caused by malevolent worms which lived inside the teeth.

The Romans cured toothaches by tying toads to their jaws.

Blood-letting, once the most profitable source of income for surgeons, became less so with the invention of a DIY blood-letting kit which allowed the patient to open a vein in the privacy of his or her own home. In the 19th century Queen Caroline of Bavaria tried it, opened up a main artery in her arm by mistake, and bled to death.

The Catholic Church helped to stifle the march of medical progress for several centuries by recognising only one expert in human anatomy, the Greek anatomist Galen, physician to the Emperor Marcus Aurelius. Although Galen's research was somewhat flawed by the fact that he'd never once seen the inside of a human body, his word on the subject was inviolable – even to question him was an act of heresy punishable by death. (When the great Belgian anatomist Andreas Vesalius correctly observed that blood flowed from the heart into the lungs, he was declared a heretic.) Galen was forced to make wild guesses based on the only material available to him – mostly dead pets and farm livestock: if it worked for dogs and pigs, it should work for humans too. Thus generations of medical students were taught that the brain was a large clot of phlegm, that the heart had two chambers, that a headache was cured by cutting holes in the skull, that the quickest way to cure a cough was to amputate the uvula at the back of the patient's palate, and that post-operative wounds should be dressed with pigeon's blood. Long after Galen's death, whenever curious surgeons insisted on doing their own anatomical research, popes and emperors would grant extremely rare permission for the odd criminal to be exhumed and cut open. The dissection had to be performed by a servant, while a doctor stood and solemnly read from the works of Galen and pointed to the parts described. When it became obvious, as it usually did, that Galen had got it completely wrong, his errors were explained away with the assertion that the corpse was 'abnormal'.

A United States Senate investigation in 1974 found that 'cowboy' surgeons were responsible for more fatalities than the annual death toll during the wars in Korea and Vietnam.

The classic cure for brewer's droop was to burn together the livers of a frog and a hedgehog, place the ashes in a bag and carry the bag about your person.

A 20th-century trepanation movement was founded by a Dutchman Dr Bart Huges, who in the 1960s figured out that a person's peace of mind was related to the amount of blood swilling around in the brain. He promptly cut a hole in his own head with an electrical drill to achieve 'a permanent high', then wrote a book about it called *Bore Hole*. The medical and legal authorities were so impressed by his discovery that they rewarded him with a spell in a Dutch lunatic asylum. Dr Huges did in fact manage to attract two converts to his cause, the London couple Joey Mellen and Amanda Fielding. After failing to find a member of the medical profession to do it for them, they finally managed to drill holes in their own heads with the help of an electric drill and generous quantities of LSD after several abortive attempts with a hand-worked corkscrew and a saw.

On 20 January 1984, David Carver, of Torquay, Devon was operated upon for the removal of a hare-lip, thus completing his 31st year on an NHS waiting list.

At one time, human urine was rubbed into the gums to relieve toothache.

Horrific pioneer attempts at blood transfusion were made in the 17th century long before it dawned on anyone that blood type compatibility was important. On 23 November 1667 members of the Royal Society gathered to witness the transfusion of twelve ounces of sheep's blood into the unfortunate Reverend Arthur Coga. Samuel Pepys recorded in his diary: 'The patient speaks well, saying that he finds himself much better, as a new man . . . but he is cracked a little in his head.'

In the European Middle Ages it was fashionable to eat and rub into the body bits of ancient Egyptian mummy for medicinal purposes. The body parts of decomposing Egyptians were widely touted as a cure for abscesses, fractures, contusions, paralysis, migraine, epilepsy, sore throats, nausea, disorders of the liver and spleen and internal ulcers. In the early part of this century some Arab tribes were still using mummies to prevent haemorrhaging. Mummy trafficking became a lucrative and highly organised business, starting in the Egyptian tombs and following a well-planned route to Europe. The bottom finally fell out of the mummy market in the late 17th century when people found out that unscrupulous dealers were selling 'fake' mummy made from recently murdered slaves.

A drop of the red stuff

The most popular cure for leprosy in the Middle Ages was to bathe in the blood of a dog. If a dog wasn't available, a two-year-old infant would do.

In ancient Rome, where human blood was prescribed as a cure for epilepsy, epileptics hung around near the exit gates of the public arenas so they could drink the blood of slain gladiators as they were dragged out. Elizabethan medical text books recommended an alternative remedy – powdered human skull dissolved in red wine.

Before the discovery of anaesthetics, when the two key qualifications for a good surgeon were quick hands and an iron stomach, it was a close call who suffered the most, surgeon or patient: at least the patient could look forward to playing with his gangrene. Most surgeons were humane men who didn't harbour any delusions about the appalling pain they inflicted on their patients. The most accomplished English surgeon of his day Sir Astley Cooper once burst into tears when a child patient smiled confidently at him just as he was about to operate. Queen Caroline's personal surgeon William Chiselden threw up before every operation, and always armed his assistant with a watch to try to keep the duration of his operations down to under three minutes. Although many operations took about an hour, Napoleon's famous chief surgeon Dominique Lorrey could amputate a leg in under 15 seconds. The 19th century Scottish surgeon and part-time bodysnatcher Robert Lister was described as 'the finest surgeon in Europe'. Lister's personal best for a leg amputation was 28 seconds, although while achieving this record he accidentally cut two of his assistant's fingers off and the patient's left testicle.

The heaviest object ever found in a human stomach was a 5lb 3oz ball of hair, extracted from a woman in the South Devon and East Cornwall Hospital in 1985.

The diarist Samuel Pepys experienced the only internal surgical operation available before the 19th century – lithotomy, or removal of a bladder stone. Pepys was trussed on his back with wrists tied to ankles, while the surgeon probed his urethra with a catheter, following it with a broader probe to locate the stone. A large cut was made near the patient's groin, then the surgeon cut through the perineum and, reaching into the bladder, extracted the stone. The operation took at least one hour and nearly half of all patients didn't survive it. Pepys was only 22 years old when he was operated on for a stone 'as big as a tennis ball' by the leading lithotomist,

Thomas Holister. Pepys was quite happy with the outcome of the operation, although it left him sterile and afterwards he often passed 'gravel' in his urine, which he tried to cure by drinking neat turpentine. He eventually died of chronic inflammation of the kidneys and urinary poisoning.

Nearly half of all children born in Great Britain in the 18th century didn't make it through infancy – a statistic which is less surprising in the light of some of the contemporary ideas about childcare. Any child who survived the shock of birth stood a good chance of reaching its first birthday if it also had the digestive system of an ox. The best-selling infant cure-all of the day 'Godfrey's Cordial' was made mostly from opium and was almost as deadly as arsenic. Children were regularly wormed with strong purgatives – a favourite was made from tepid milk mixed with equal quantities of fine sugar and rat's dung.

Early suggested cures for syphilis included intercourse with a virgin, rubbing dung into the male organ, and bathing in horse urine. The only regular precaution taken to avoid venereal disease in Elizabethan times was the washing of genitals in vinegar. Eighteenth-century cures for venereal disease included a sound thrashing, or having the penis wrapped in the warm parts of a freshly dismembered fowl.

If not for a much-publicised test case in 1731, human vivisection may have flourished legally during the 18th century. When William Chiselden was appointed surgeon to Queen Caroline one of his first tasks was to find a cure for her profound deafness. He attempted to secure a human guinea pig in the form of a convicted criminal named Rey: the deal was that Rey would go free, and in return Chiselden would be allowed to do unspeakable things to Rey's ears, i.e. deafen him then bore holes in his ears to find out if perforation would be of any value to the royal earhole. There was a huge outcry by right-wing Hanoverians, but not on humanitarian grounds. They argued that vivisection was too good for Rey and he shouldn't be allowed to cheat the gallows: in any case, Rey might escape while he was in Chiselden's custody. The authorities bowed to the pressure and Chiselden was ordered to confine his experiments to the dead. The surgeon may yet have had his own way: he eventually helped establish the Company of Surgeons, whose headquarters were suspiciously located next door to Newgate Prison.

Midwifery was once the sole privilege of women and men were forbidden to attend. A Hamburg doctor name Wertt who wanted to learn more about obstetrics managed to observe several childbirths by dressing as a woman. When his real identity was exposed he was burned at the stake.

In ancient Greece the preferred method of hastening childbirth was to either lift the pregnant woman and repeatedly drop her onto a couch, or to strap the woman to a couch, turn it upright, then pound it repeatedly onto a bundle of faggots.

A book called *Anatomy of Melancholy*, written by Robert Burton, became the authoritative work on the subject of mental illness when it was published in 1621. He taught that madness was often caused by the retention of bodily excretions: the best cure was to tie patients to a wall and literally beat the crap out of them.

The standard text on the subject of madness for most of the 19th century was written by the top French physician Jean Esquirol. Mental illness, said Esquirol, was caused by living in a new home, squeezing a pimple, old age, childbirth, the menstrual cycle, a blow on the head, constipation, shrinkage of haemorrhoids, misuse of mercury, disappointment in love, political upheavals, shock, thwarted ambition, excessive study, masturbation, prostitution, religion and bloodletting. Confusingly, bloodletting was at the time also considered to be one of the best cures for madness.

Until the 20th century most English doctors were taught that much mental illness was a result of large quantities of phlegm. The standard course of treatment was to force the patient to be violently sick three or four times a day.

The 'mad' King George III's treatment was in accordance with the standard treatment: 'restraint, frequent but moderate bleedings, purges (forced vomiting or emetics), a low diet, salivations, and afterwards the cold bath'. The King's condition turned out to be a goldmine for the medical profession: he was visited by a succession of quacks who hoped to make their fortune by finding a cure for his affliction. The most notorious of these was the Reverend Dr Francis Willis, who diagnosed the King's illness as arising from 'severe exercise, weighty business, severe abstemiousness and too little rest'. George III had occasional remissions from his condition, and in 1789 official medals were struck to celebrate his 'recovery'. Dr Willis meanwhile had some of his own struck for advertising purposes. On one side of the medallion there was a head and shoulders view of the physician, while the other bore the legend, 'Britons rejoice Your King's Restored – 1789'.

When Charles II had a fit while shaving in 1685, he was lucky to be treated with the finest medical advice of the day. He was attended by fourteen physicians who first drew blood, forced him to vomit violently then gave him a strong laxative. They shaved his head, applied blistering agents to his scalp, put special plasters made from pigeon droppings onto the soles of his feet, fed him bezoar stones (usually found in the gall bladder of a goat) and made him drink 40 drops of extract from a dead man's skull. He died two days later.

John Hunter, the unrivalled expert of 18th-century anatomy, may have been either the bravest or the most foolhardy surgeon who ever lived. In order to study venereal disease he deliberately injected himself with pus from a gonorrhoea patient who, unknown to Hunter, also had syphilis. The experiment cost him his life. Like many of his fellow anatomists, Hunter collected the corpses of executed criminals for dissection. His prize exhibit was the body of a 7ft 8in Irishman, Charles Byrne, which he had acquired in spite of stiff competition from a number of local anatomists who were keen to lay their hands on the Irish 'giant'. Byrne meanwhile lived with a dread fear that he might end up in a museum, and made special arrangements to be buried at sea in a lead coffin. When he finally died of tuberculosis, however, Hunter bribed officials to fill the coffin with rocks and gave them £500 for the corpse. Hunter was intensely proud of his latest plaything. He propped the corpse up beside him on his coach while doing his rounds, then took it home and boiled it in a large vat to separate the flesh from the bones.

John Hunter's brother William was also an anatomist who specialised in the collection of female corpses in various states of pregnancy. In total he dissected between 300 and 400. As pregnant women were never, ever executed, none of his specimens could have been acquired legally.

When radiation was first discovered in the 19th century it was immediately pronounced to be as harmless and beneficial as sunshine, and so began a medical craze for radiation treatment of the most trivial ailments. For a period of around 40 years into the early part of this century large numbers of people were needlessly exposed to lethal doses of radiation for such minor problems as ringworm and acne: women were treated for post-natal depression by having their ovaries irradiated.

In 1819 the Glasgow surgeon Dr James Jeffrey attended a public demonstration of galvanism – the study of the effects of electrical currents passed through the human body – by a fellow lecturer Andrew Ure. The body was that of a collier, Matthew Clydesdale, who had been hanged for murder and, in accordance with the law of the day, his warm corpse handed over to medical students. Before a packed audience of students and members of the public, Clydesdale was seated in a chair and his hands were attached to a battery. As the current was switched on, the horrified spectators saw the man's chest suddenly heave and the body stand upright. Dr Jeffrey coolly saved the day by expertly slitting the man's throat with a scalpel. Although Jeffrey had technically committed murder, he was never charged because the man had already been executed and was therefore legally dead. This was to be the very last time in Britain that anyone was allowed to stage a public anatomical dissection of a human body or to experiment with electricity on corpses.

The 18th-century equivalent of the proverb 'an apple a day keeps the doctor away', was 'live right, piss light'.

Quacks specialising in uroscopy, commonly known as Piss Prophets, made fortunes out of the gullible public, claiming the ability to accurately diagnose illness by staring at, then testing, a sample of the patient's urine. Since the medical establishment hadn't a clue what a patient's urine did, or did not reveal about illness, there was nothing to stop them taking thousands of people for a ride.

Britain's all-time most successful quack was Joshua Ward, who operated in London in the 18th century and could claim George II as one of his satisfied patients. He made a fortune from selling his famous Ward's Pill, which he advertised as a cure-all for almost every infirmity from scurvy to heart disease and mental illness. The ingredients of the miraculous Pill were kept a secret until his death, which was just as well for Ward. It was in fact made from antimony, a toxic metal which if taken regularly causes fatty degeneration of the liver, gastro-enteritis, inflammation of the kidneys and the colon and eventual death from shock and circulatory collapse.

When Prince Henry, eldest son of James I, lay dying with typhus, his doctor prescribed a treatment of having pigeons pecking at the soles of his feet. James I also picked up a few useful remedies of his own: after a hard day in the saddle he liked nothing more than to relax with his legs immersed in the bowels of a dead stag – nothing better for strengthening the sinews.

THAT'S ENTERTAINMENT

The lead singer of Milwaukee rock band the Toilet Rockers was convicted of disorderly conduct in 1991 after exercising what he claimed was his 'constitutional right' to defecate onstage and fling his turds at the audience.

Black Sabbath's lead singer Ozzie Osborne really did bite off the head of a dead bat, but it wasn't deliberate. He thought that the ex-mammal, thrown on stage by a fan, was a rubber toy. He said, 'It was like eating a Crunchie wrapped in chamois leather.'

Next to sex and gluttony, Elvis's other favourite nocturnal pastime was visiting the Memphis morgue to view the corpses.

The whipping of semi-naked female prisoners at London's Brideswell prison in the 18th century was so popular that a special gallery was constructed for spectators.

The American showman Phineas T. Barnum exploited dozens of freaks throughout his career but none more shamelessly than Joice Heth, a poor old blind and semi-paralysed black woman who Barnum advertised as 'nurse to General George Washington . . . now at the astonishing age of 161 years'. In fact she was only 80 years old but looked much older, and Barnum had acquired her from a sideshow in Philadelphia. When Joice Heth died in 1836 he found another way of making money from the poor woman – he hired a leading pathologist to perform an autopsy on her in front of a paying audience.

In 1889 Thomas Cook's travel agency organised a package tour to watch the executions by guillotine of Messrs Allorto and Sellier. He filled 300 seats on a chartered fleet of horse-buses.

A church in the Czechoslovakian town of Sedlec has a chandelier made entirely of human bones.

It isn't coincidental that the regulation soccer ball is roughly the size of a man's head. The first football used in England was the head of a dead Danish brigand.

The Sicilian Frank Lentini was probably the world's biggest crowd-pulling sideshow freak. The 'King of Freaks' was the result of non-separating triplets, which left him with three legs, two sets of genitals and four feet.

Illegal gamblers in Manila often have corpses sitting in on their card games. The Philippino police have a habit of busting gambling dens and demanding bribes to allow the game to continue, but because most of them are devoutly Catholic they would never raid a wake or a funeral. The gamblers usually buy the bodies from the unclaimed corpse section of the local mortuary.

In ancient Rome members of the showbiz fraternity were expected to wear rings through holes pierced in their foreskins to discourage them from taking advantage of female groupies.

The average Briton will spend two years of his or her life watching TV advertisements.

The Polish-born US sprint champion Stella Walsh was one of the most exciting and most successful athletes of the 1930s – the first woman ever to beat 11 seconds in the 100 yards sprint and the winner of 41 amateur athletics titles and two Olympic Gold medals. Nearly half a century later Stella Walsh hit the headlines again: in 1980 the former sprint champion was an innocent by-stander at a Cleveland bank robbery attempt, when she was shot dead. The autopsy revealed that 'she' was a man. The woman's champion downhill ski-racer of 1966 Erika Schineggar was revealed to be a man after a chromosome test in 1967. She later changed her name to Eric and became a successful husband and father. The 1946 French relay team had two members of suspect gender,

Claire Bresolles and Lea Caulon. After their retirement from athletics they lived their lives as Pierre and Leon. After the German Olympic high jumper Dora Ratjen won the European championships with a world record-breaking 5ft 7ins, she became a waiter called Hermann.

The deadliest ever ball game was Tlachtli, played in the Middle Ages by the Maya Indians of Central America. Two teams struggled violently to force a rubber ball through their opponents' goal – vertical stone rings on elevated pedestals at either end of the court. Players often died during the game. The losing team's players were decapitated and their heads put on display.

Rat killing was one of the most popular spectator sports for the Victorian gentleman. For one shilling he could watch and place bets on dozens of dogs as they ripped their way through hundreds of live rats in a large pit. The winning dog, i.e. the one who destroyed the largest number of rats, received a special collar and a cash prize for the owner. The record was held by a dog who killed 500 rats in less than six minutes. The dogs usually suffered appalling injuries as a result of savage rat bites, usually to the mouth and muzzle.

In the 18th century, Surgeons' Hall in London was regularly decorated with the dead bodies of executed murderers for public viewing. Not surprisingly, naked corpses attracted voyeurs: *The Times* reported with distaste that women had queued to see the naked corpse of a reputedly well-endowed killer who had robbed and murdered a servant girl then enjoyed a three-in-a-bed romp with the corpse and his girlfriend.

The Vatican's most outrageous party was thrown by Pope Alexander VI in 1501. As he and his teenage mistress watched, 50 naked whores recruited from the city slums were required to slither around on his marble floor picking up chestnuts with their labia. It became known as the 'chestnut supper'.

The term 'gala day' derives from the gruesome 18th-century custom of declaring public holidays during notable executions at Tyburn (now Marble Arch) in London, to entertain the mob. These occasions were originally known as 'gallows days'. In total, about 60,000 people were put to death at Tyburn.

The Seattle-based Jim Rose Alternative Circus has the world's most tasteless speciality acts. Their star turn is Matt Cowley, who entertains people by sticking 47ft of tubing up his nose and into his gut, then pumping a mixture of beer, chocolate and ketchup into his stomach. The resulting green mixture of 'bile beer' is then pumped back out again and offered to a member of the audience for consumption. Another Alternative Circus favourite is the transvestite Mr Lifto, who perforates his foreskin with a coat hanger, then suspends weights from it.

Watching the insane at the Royal Bethlehem (Bedlam)

Hospital in the 18th century was the latter-day equivalent of a day out at London Zoo. Spectators flocked to buy tickets from the Hospital so they could watch the mentally ill cavort. Hospital records for 1779 noted that some visitors were abusing the system, and it was decided that the words 'and three friends' should be printed on the invitations to limit the numbers to four per ticket. At the Hospice de Charenton lunatic asylum in northern France, the inmates were made to wear fancy-dress costume and perform for the amusement of paying customers.

Sport's first ever sex test, carried out by the International Athletics Association in 1965, required women athletes to parade naked in front of a panel of five gynaecologists. Five Russian champion athletes, including the famous 'sisters' Irena and Tamara Press, went into immediate retirement.

When King Louis XI of France, noted for his sick sense of humour and bizarre whims, once demanded to be entertained by 'a consort of swine voices', opportunity knocked for the Abbot of Baigne, France's only entertainer on the novelty pig organ. The abbot laid a range of pigs out side by side, and when he struck the organ keys small spikes would prick the pigs, causing them to squeal 'in such an order and consonance as highly delighted the king and all his company'.

Jim Morrison of The Doors was found guilty of exposure

after asking his audience one evening, 'Do you want to see my cock?'

In the Philippines Barry Manilow is worshipped like a god. In 1983 50,000 adoring Filipinos paid to see him perform five nights running, and his albums are even bootlegged.

A few words about flatulence . . .
The virtuoso of the anal accordion was the French baker Joseph Pujol, who earned fame and fortune at the turn of the century as Le Pétomane, or roughly translated, 'the manic farter'. At an early age Pujol made two remarkable discoveries while lying in his bath-tub: the second was that he could control the intake of water into his body by contracting his abdominal muscles. At first Pujol began to put his supernatural sphincter to good use by demonstrating a unique water spouting act. Once he had discovered that he could also not only control air in the same way, but that he could actually modulate sound with completely odourless farting, he never looked back. Pujol took his act to Paris where he became an overnight sensation, outselling even France's favourite actress Sarah Bernhardt. His act included a series of imitations including the sound of calico being torn, a cannon, an eight-day-old pup, a creaking door, an owl hooting, a duck, a swarm of bees, a bullfrog, and a pig. He could play, by placing a small flute in his rectum, 'By The Light Of The Moon', and could anally extinguish a candle at a distance of one foot. For an encore Pujol would insert a

yard of rubber hosing with a cigarette in one end into his rectum, then draw on the cigarette and exhale smoke. The highlight of Pujol's spectacular career was a continental tour which drew many of the crowned heads of Europe – although King Leopold II of Belgium felt obliged to see his show in disguise. His career ended with World War I, and he went back to baking. Pujol died in 1945 aged 88.

The only legitimate European female *pétomane* (i.e. one who performed without mechanical aids such as bellows concealed beneath her skirts) was a lady known as La Mère Alexandre, whose act was proudly billed as 'without trickery or odour'. Mme Alexandre's anal dexterity was such that she could imitate the farts of the famous, and perform a series of entertaining 'occupational farts' including nuns and freemasons. Her magnum opus however was her impression of the bombardment of Port Arthur.

A 1980s American *pétomane* and part-time stripper known as Honeysuckle Divine could extinguish a candle flame at two paces and could fart 'Jingle Bells'.

Japan's answer to Le Pétomane appeared on TV in 1980 claiming he could break wind 3,000 times in succession. He took off his pants and lay on the studio floor while the compere held the microphone in a suitable position. He could also apply a blowgun to his rectum and, accompanied by a studio orchestra, accurately fire darts into a target.

SKIN DEEP

Although Napoleon's Josephine was the subject of many highly flattering portraits, she was not a great beauty. Josephine was six years Napoleon's senior and, according to a contemporary, the Duchesse d'Abrantes, 'her teeth were frightfully bad, but when her mouth was shut she had the appearance, especially at a few paces distant, of a young and pretty woman'.

The 17th-century Hungarian lesbian Countess Elizabeth de B'athory scorned the more traditional moisturisers and anti-wrinkle creams, preferring to bathe in warm virgin's blood. To maintain a regular supply she slaughtered more than 650 girls.

Excrement was once widely used as a beauty treatment, and in some parts of the world still is. Hare dung was a cure for sagging breasts: camel dung was rubbed into the scalp to make the hair wavy. Ass or hen dung was used to cure skin blemishes, swellings or burns.

George Washington had at least four sets of false teeth which he soaked in port overnight because it made them taste better. His dentures were variously made from ivory, lead, and the teeth of humans, cows, hippopotami and walrus. Washington was also noted for never smiling much for his portraits.

The longest recorded female beard belonged to Janice Deveree of Kentucky, who in 1842 sported a 14-inch goatee.

The distinguished scientist Sir Francis Galbon, who invented identikit photos, fingerprinting and the science of eugenics, also invented a pocket counting device which he used to clock the number of attractive women he passed in the street. After many years of dedicated research Galbon's instrument helped him to compile a 'beauty map' of Great Britain, which ventured to prove that Britain's ugliest women lived in Aberdeen. Galbon apparently went on to invent a device for measuring the size of African female bottoms.

Vax Pox
Nine-tenths of ordinary household dust is dead human skin. Every seven years you can literally claim to be a new you because your outer covering will have completely replaced itself: the old you is in the Hoover bag. You will shed about 40lb of dead skin in a lifetime.

Dog urine was promoted as the Tudor equivalent of Grecian 2000. Horse urine rubbed into the scalp reduced hair loss: a pint of cow urine a day promoted healthy skin. The drinking of human urine was recommended to improve virility.

When Queen Elizabeth I finally lost all of her teeth she took to stuffing layers of cloth under her lips to fill out her face.

Men's fashion in mediaeval Europe dictated that high-ranking noblemen should expose their naked genitals below short-fitting tunics. If the genitals weren't big enough a chap could wear padded flesh-coloured falsies, or braquettes. Edward VI passed a law banning any man below the rank of lord from exposing 'his privy member and buttokkes' in 1548.

The first nose-jobs were performed 2,000 years ago by amateur Hindu surgeons with often gruesome results. Cutting off noses was a common punishment for theft.

The great 16th-century Danish astronomer Tycho Brahe wore an artificial nose made from silver and gold.

During the reign of Elizabeth I the Church proclaimed that any woman found guilty of 'leading a subject of her majesty into marriage' by wearing cosmetics, make-up or high-heeled shoes should be burned as a witch. This was an unusual ruling, given that the Queen herself was a prolific cosmetics abuser, especially in her later years. According to the fashion of the day unmarried women wore their breasts exposed – a habit Elizabeth favoured well into her seventies. Her breasts were heavily pow-dered and covered in ceruse, the popular lead-based whitener which scarred and poisoned the women of northern Europe for centuries, and her veins were highlighted with blue dye.

Eighteenth-century French women used to eat arsenic wafers to make their skin fashionably pallid.

Many modern skin creams and beauty treatments contain extracts of cows' brains, sheep's spleens, spinal cord and stomach lining, and foetal cells from calves. Some up-market perfumes contain ambergris – a product of the sperm whale – and civet, which is extracted from the sex glands of the civet cat.

Early British dentures were mounted sets of human teeth extracted from corpses. 'Toothing' in the early 19th century was big business, and the teeth of the dead became valuable commodities. Many bodysnatchers took to 'toothing' as a lucrative way to spend their spare time. In 1808 two of England's most notorious bodysnatchers, the prize-fighter and gangleader Ben Crouch and his side-kick Daniel Butler went on a 'busman's holiday' to the Peninsular War to collect teeth from corpses on the battlefield. Teeth from the dead of the American Civil War were shipped to England to be worn by the rich and the fashionable.

In 1911 an American mail order con netted hundreds of thousands of dollars with the promise of a miracle treatment that could turn blacks into whites.

Ancient Roman commanders forced dogs to swallow metal tubes containing messages, which they then had to deliver. When the dogs reached their destination they were killed and their bellies slit open to retrieve the messages.

The top brand name beauty lotion of the 16th century was Soliman, or Soliman's Water, which was applied to the skin to eliminate spots, freckles and warts. It certainly did the job, although a girl might as well have applied a blowtorch to her face with less horrific consequences. The chief ingredient of this lotion was mercury, which burned away the outer layers of skin and corroded the flesh underneath. One side effect was that the girl's teeth fell out even more quickly than was usual at this time: her gums receded and by the age of 30 the user would be a rotting wreck.

The Chinese believed that they could prevent hair loss by eating rat flesh.

Until Edward Jenner found a cure for it by deliberately infecting a small boy with the fluid from cowpox blisters then exposing him to infectious victims – not one of the most ethical experiments in medical history – smallpox was the biggest killer mankind had ever known. The description 'fair' didn't normally apply, as it does today, to people with blond hair. It was used to describe a complexion unscarred by smallpox – virtually everyone else was hideously marked by the pustular rash.

At the end of the 17th century it was the fashion for women to have their gums pierced with hooks to keep their dentures in place.

In the smallpox-ravaged 17th century, 'complexion milks' were all the rage. The favourite was a mixture of dung, minced veal and goat hair mixed with lemon juice, milk or cucumber water. Not surprisingly they didn't improve complexions which remained scarred, sallow and spotty. Most women who could afford them took to wearing masks out of doors.

In the 1920s beauty parlours all over the US installed X-ray equipment to remove unwanted facial and body hair. Radiation was touted as a cure-all for every imaginable disease: products available included radioactive toothpaste for whiter teeth and better digestion, radioactive face creams to lighten the skin, even radium-laced chocolate bars. A brisk trade in radioactive patent medicines thrived well into the 1930s. One of the most popular preparations was radium water, promoted in the United States as a general tonic and known as 'liquid sunshine'. It was responsible for the deaths of several thousand people. In 1932 Frederick Godfrey the 'well-known British Hair Specialist' was advertising a radioactive hair tonic, and as late as 1953 a company in Denver was promoting a radium-based contraceptive jelly.

Artificial dentures were invented at the end of the 19th century by an English dentist who disliked handling the teeth of dead men. For a while cheap celluloid teeth were popular: they never really caught on because they were highly inflammable and prone to bursting into flames if you smoked.

The most ruthless French revolutionary Jean Paul Marat
had to spend most of his time in the bath to obtain relief
from a number of painful and disfiguring skin diseases
picked up during the years he spent hiding in cellars and
sewers. He also met his death in his bathtub when
Charlotte Corday severed the aorta near his heart with a
sharpened table knife.

No one ever accused Tory MPs of being handsome, but
Joseph Biggar, the 19th-century parliamentarian who
invented 'obstruction' and brought about the Commons
guillotine, is said to have been the ugliest ever. Biggar
had a hunchback, a grating voice, a speech impediment,
a 'face like a gargoyle', bony hands and abnormally large
feet. He also took to wearing in the Commons a bizarre
foul-smelling waistcoat fashioned from an unknown
species of animal skin. When Biggar rose to make his
maiden speech, a startled Benjamin Disraeli turned to
a colleague and said, 'What's that?'

The French cosmetic manufacturer Roc markets three
beauty treatments which contain human placenta collected from French maternity hospitals.

The ugliest woman in history is said to have been one
Julia Pastrana, a Mexican who lived in the mid-1800s.
She was ruthlessly exploited by her manager, who
married her to ensure that he had sole rights of owner-
ship, then turned her into an international freak-show

exhibit. When she became pregnant he made a small fortune by selling tickets to the birth. The deformed child died stillborn and the mother died soon afterwards. For her husband the grief of losing his family came a poor second to the shock of losing his livelihood. He had mother and child embalmed, placed in a glass case, and shunted off on a lucrative world tour.

The origin of the sexist 'paper bag' joke was probably the unfortunate Miss Tannakin Skinker, who lived in northern Germany in the early to mid-17th century. She was born to wealthy parents, and had a perfectly normal body, but hog-like features which earned her the unflattering nickname 'the pig-faced lady'. The girl's deformity was kept a secret by her parents for years, but eventually news of her condition leaked out and a flood of voyeurs flocked to the family home. Against all odds her family tried to increase her eligibility rating by dressing their daughter in the finest and most expensive clothing and throwing in a dowry of about £40,000. One young man, undaunted by the stories circulated by people who had seen the girl, commented, 'put her head in a blacke bagge and what difference between her and another woman?' As soon her veil was lifted however he went the same way as all the other enterprising suitors and ran away in horror. Miss Tannakin lived out her days as a single woman.

When Liberace had his final face lift the plastic surgeon accidentally removed so much wrinkled skin from his patient's face that Liberace could no longer keep his eyes closed, even when asleep. He had to use eyedrops throughout the night to keep his eyeballs from drying up. Liberace later had the face of his male lover reconstructed by plastic surgery to make him look like the celebrity's twin.

Soldiers of the Cheshire regiment in World War I had such bad teeth they were supplied with small mincers to help them eat their food.

Physiognomy is the ancient science of judging a person's character by his appearance. A Greek physiognomist once deduced from the uncannily pig-like features of the philosopher Socrates that he was a drunkard and a brute. When Socrates' followers violently objected to this, the great man intervened and announced that the reading was, in fact, quite correct.

R.I.P.

Apart from prostitution, undertaking is the world's most recession-proof industry. The world's largest undertaking business, Services Corporation International of Houston, Texas, has an annual turnover of around $600 million.

Although Thomas Hardy expressed a dying wish that his last resting place be at his birthplace in Stinsford, the authorities decreed that he was much too important for such an anonymous interment. It was decided that his remains be sent to Westminster Abbey: only Hardy's heart could be buried at his birthplace. According to legend, on the morning of the ceremony his sister inadvertently left the open casket on the kitchen table and the contents were greedily consumed by the Hardy family cat.

Lenin has been a poor conversationalist since 1924 but the world's most famous embalmee has still managed to get through several dozen new suits. Twice a week the parts that show (i.e. his hands and face) are painted with fresh embalming fluid, and every eighteen months the whole body is lifted out and given a thoroughly good soaking. Every four years a bit of Lenin is scraped off, placed under a microscope and examined for signs of deterioration. This hasn't allayed a widely held suspicion among Muscovites that the city's longest running show is in fact a straw body and a waxwork head.

In 1976 a 'dummy' corpse hanging by a noose in a Long Beach, California Amusement Park turned out to be the real thing. The figure had been part of a fun-house exhibit for five years until officials at the park made their gruesome discovery during the filming of an episode of the *Six Million Dollar Man* TV series. A cameraman was busily adjusting the arm when it fell off, revealing a protruding human bone. The corpse, wrapped in gauze and sprayed with paint, had been bought by the amusement park from a local wax museum, and was never identified.

So great was the dread of premature burial in the 19th century that over 200 books were written on the subject, and societies were formed to prevent it. The writer Harriet Martineau left her doctor £10 with instructions that he should make sure she was well and truly deceased before her burial by cutting her head off. The novelist Edmund Yates similarly left a 20-guinea fee for any surgeon kind enough to slit his jugular vein before interment. The novelist Wilkie Collins always carried a letter with him, imploring anyone finding him 'dead' to

contact the nearest doctor for a second opinion. Colonel
Edward Vollun of the US Army Medical Corps offered a
more practical solution. Anyone buried without an autopsy, suggested the Colonel, should be interred with a
bottle of chloroform within easy reach so that if that
person should find himself in the unfortunate situation
of being buried alive, he could commit suicide with the
minimum fuss.

The Russian Czar Peter the Great kept the head of his
wife's lover pickled in alcohol in a bedside jar.

The 'processing' of human corpses to create raw material
was a British, not a Nazi, invention. On 18 November
1822 the *Observer* reported that the Napoleonic battle-
fields of Leipzig, Austerlitz and Waterloo had been
'swept alike of the bones of the hero and of the horse
which he rode' and hundreds of tons of the bones had
been shipped to Yorkshire bone-grinders to make fertili-
sers for farmers. After the siege of Plevna in 1877 a local
newspaper farming column casually reported that,
'thirty tons of human bones, comprising thirty thousand
skeletons, have just landed at Bristol from Plevna'.

Dr Johnson wrote *Rasselas* in seven days flat to pay for
his mother's funeral.

Until 1788 bodysnatching was not a criminal offence:
you could however be prosecuted for the theft of the
coffin. The undisputed king of the English bodysnatching fraternity was Ben Crouch, who made and lost a

fortune from his sales of stiffs to London surgeons. After a long career Crouch was finally found dead sitting upright in a bar near Tower Hill, London.

During the 'golden age of bodysnatching' in early 19th-century Britain, the going rate for a corpse was two to three guineas for a body over three feet long, and a guinea or less for dead children or tiny babies, known respectively in the trade as 'large smalls' and 'foetuses'.

No fool like a cold fool

An American company which promises immortality through cryogenics offers to keep you hanging around in a vat of liquid nitrogen until a cure is found for a mere $100,000. For less wealthy optimists they also do a 'budget' deal: a mere $35,000 will entitle you to have only your head frozen. The company claims that your head contains important genes and memory cells from which the rest of the body can be regrown.

When he wasn't philosophising, the Elizabethan, Francis Bacon spent his spare time pondering on the problem of how to preserve bodies after death. One winter's day while Bacon was riding through Highgate in London, he saw a chicken. Bacon jumped out of his carriage, wrung the bird's neck and stuffed the carcass with snow. The experiment was an unqualified success: sadly Bacon contracted a fatal chill in the process and died four weeks later.

Leonardo da Vinci was a sodomiser of boys and a grave-robber. Until Pope Leo X put a stop to it, Leonardo

da Vinci dissected more than 100 corpses. His resurrec-
tionist activities were undiscovered until the beginning of
this century when his secret, unpublished anatomical
studies were revealed for the first time. His Mona Lisa
and his John the Baptist, which feature the same model,
may have both been self-portraits.

Until the second half of this century, coffins were rarely
made to measure. If the body didn't fit the coffin the
undertaker would normally break the corpse's ankles
and bend the feet back.

The 19th-century Sussex MP John 'Mad Jack' Fuller
(1752–1834), builder of follies, declined a conventional
burial because of his morbid fear of being eaten by his
own relatives. Fuller reasoned, 'the worms would eat
me, the duck would eat the worms, and my relatives
would eat the ducks'. He had a pyramid-shaped mausoleum constructed in which he sat in an armchair wearing a top hat and holding a glass of claret.

The author, poet and soldier Robert Graves achieved a
unique 'double' when he survived World War I and his
own obituary. In 1916 Graves was badly wounded in
France and left for dead. He was found alive but
unconscious the following day, and was taken to hospital. By that time however the army's well-oiled bereave-
ment system had already written him off, and his

distraught mother was informed that her son had been killed in action. She received the standard letter of condolences, and an announcement was made in *The Times*. Graves responded with his own formal announcement in *The Times*, informing friends that he was recovering nicely from the wounds which had recently killed him. Graves was highly amused to find that some of his worst enemies had written fond tributes to his mother about him.

During the reign of Constantine the Great, one of the very few grounds on which a woman could obtain a divorce was if her husband was a grave-robber.

Until 1824 suicides were banned from burial in consecrated ground, and were buried instead at a crossroads with a stake through the heart. The belief was that suicides returned as malicious ghosts unless they were tethered to one spot by a stake. If the spirit did get free, the choice of roads would confuse it.

The 10th Duke of Hamilton, Alexander Douglas outbid the British Museum when he paid £11,000 for a magnificent ancient tomb which had been originally made for an Egyptian princess. Douglas housed it in a fabulous mausoleum at his ancestral home, Hamilton Palace. It wasn't until his death in 1852 that it was discovered that he was too tall to fit inside it: the only way they could get him in was by sawing his feet off.

In 1950 the philosopher and reformer Jeremy Bentham

had his first change of underwear in 100 years. Bentham had a theory that the bodies of people could be put to practical use. He argued that every man, if properly embalmed, could be used as his own statue or 'auto-icon'. The possibilities were endless: portraits of ancestors could be replaced by actual heads. '. . . many generations being deposited on a few shelves or in a modest sized cupboard'. When Bentham died he had left instructions that his own body be dissected for the benefit of medical science, them embalmed, dressed in his own clothes, and placed in a glass case. His head however had to be replaced by a wax version because his expression lost a certain something during the embalming process. Bentham's physician Dr Southwood Smith kept the body until his own death in 1850 whereupon it was presented to University College, London, where it remains to this day.

The great leveller

For hundreds of years the dead in Britain were buried on top of one another in churchyards so that the ground level of graves eventually rose higher than the foundations of the church – a fact that can be verified by looking at almost any old churchyard today. In the last century the lack of burial space in inner cities put pressure on churchyards with often gruesome results. One London churchyard of less than one acre in size received 14,000 bodies over a period of 20 years. Undertakers often had to store the corpses of stillborn children in their own homes until they had collected enough to justify digging a hole for mass burial.

A freak storm in the early 1980s washed up more than 100 coffins from a local cemetery in Verdugo Hills, Los Angeles, and onto the city streets. Rotting coffins were swept along on the crest of a mudslide, plunging corpses, some of which had been buried for decades, through windows and into houses and stores. A local newspaper photographer found one body wedged upright in the doorway of a supermarket.

By 1869 so few natives survived in Tasmania that when William Lanne died he became a subject of a bizarre battle between local scientists and London's Royal College of Surgeons. Both parties believed that Lanne was one of the last of his race, and each was determined to acquire the corpse for study. A doctor representing the Royal College severed Lanne's head and stole the skull, but not before craftily skinning it and substituting another skull to try to delay discovery of the theft. When the Tasmanian officials realised they had been tricked, they cut off the hands and feet to prevent the Royal College from stealing the whole skeleton. The body was buried, but later quietly exhumed by agents of the Royal College and shipped off to London. Lanne's head didn't survive the journey: it had been wrapped in leather, and was thrown overboard when the ship's crew finally found the smell too much to handle.

In November 1888 the remains of the Spanish artist Francisco Goya were exhumed from the cemetery in Bordeaux where he had lain for 60 years in order to return him to his native country for re-burial. When the coffin was opened however, Goya's head was missing. The whereabouts of Goya's head is still not known to this day.

Apart from the original proprietor, Oliver Cromwell's head had at least ten different owners. After the restoration of the monarchy on the anniversary of the execution of King Charles I, Cromwell's corpse was exhumed from Westminster Abbey and hanged at Tyburn. He was taken down, decapitated, his body was thrown into a pit beneath the gallows and the head set on a spike above Westminster Hall. The head remained there for 43 years until it was dislodged in a violent storm in 1703, and was found lying on the floor by a sentry. He took it home and kept it hidden in his chimney, and on his death left it to his daughter. In 1710 the head reappeared, this time in a freak show. By 1775 it had been sold to an actor named Russell, who in turn sold it in 1787 to James Fox, an antique dealer. Fox sold it for £230 to three men who put it on display in Old Bond Street, London and charged half a crown per viewing. By 1865 it had passed into the possession of a Mr Williamson of Beckenham. His family donated it to Sydney Sussex College in the 1960s.

In March 1978 the body of Charlie Chaplin was stolen from its grave in Vevey, Switzerland and held for a 600,000 franc ransom by a Pole, Roman Wardas, and a

Bulgarian, Gantcho Ganev. The bodysnatchers were finally arrested and Chaplin's remains were retrieved from a cornfield a few miles away. They said they needed the money to start a garage business.

In 1876 an American gang was apprehended while attempting to steal the remains of Abraham Lincoln. They planned to hold it for ransom in return for the release of a convicted forger, Ben Boyd. Lincoln's coffin was subsequently embedded in steel and concrete.

After the remains of the poet John Milton were raided by souvenir hunters at St Giles, Cripplegate in 1790, a woman gravedigger Elizabeth Grant was found to be charging visitors sixpence a time for a viewing of Milton's teeth and part of his leg.

Until the 19th century one in every three baby girls in China was killed because they were a liability to their parents – a 'useless mouth' which would contribute less to the family income than it would consume. It wasn't until greater contact with the West that the Chinese realised the value of the child prostitution market, and children who would have otherwise been quietly murdered were instead ceremoniously apprenticed to brothels.

Crucified criminals in the Roman empire were often liable, while still hanging on their crosses, to be mutilated by practitioners of black magic. Some historians claim that the body of Jesus was guarded after his death, not as Matthew suggests, to stop his disciples from taking him away, but to prevent graverobbers from despoiling the body of its extremities.

Richard I's tomb at Westminster Abbey had a hole in it, through which visitors could actually touch his skull. In 1776 a schoolboy stole the king's jawbone: it was kept as a family heirloom until it was finally returned to the Abbey in 1906.

Dead men can have 'erections' – a condition which results from bloating, with decomposition, of the sexual organs. This probably contributed to the ancient myth of the vampire, which was generally depicted as a highly sexed creature.

Not tonight, Josephine

Napoleon Bonaparte's penis, removed at his autopsy by a team of French and Belgian doctors, turned out to be a major disappointment when it was put up for auction in 1972 at Christie's and failed to reach its reserve price. It was approximately one inch long, resembled a fossilised pork scratching, and was listed as 'a small dried-up object'.

After Rasputin was variously poisoned, shot and drowned, his penis was hacked off and preserved in a small velvet-lined box.

Because of the high water content of the average human adult, cremation is extremely difficult without modern-day furnaces. In Greece and India bodies were first wrapped in layers of animal fat to aid combustion. In India many families couldn't afford enough firewood to do the job properly and half-burned bodies were regularly thrown into the river. The City of London Crematorium in Manor Park burns 4,639 corpses a year, making it Britain's busiest.

The Biami head-hunters of New Guinea never bury their dead. The corpses are left to rot on platforms in the open, and female mourners smear themselves with excrement from the bodies as a sign of respect for the deceased.

Resurrection Shuffle

Gravestones were originally intended to prevent the dead from rising. For hundreds of years gravediggers and mortuary workers have reported sightings of long-dead corpses apparently sitting up – a phenomenon due to commonplace biological, rather than supernatural, causes. The human body has its own post-death system which switches on to prepare the corpse for decomposition. The corpse contains chemicals which continue to function and cause organs to contract. Muscles and tissues within the stomach and lower digestive tract are reduced, and the body arches forward into the sitting position.

When the Russian court official Count Karnice Karnicki witnessed the premature burial of a young Belgian girl he was so shocked by the experience that he tried to patent a new type of coffin which would ensure that such a mistake never happened again. His contraption involved a long tube which extended from the coffin six feet above ground. The uppermost part of the tube led to a sealed box, while at the other end a glass ball, attached to a wire spring, was placed on the deceased's chest. The coffin was also fitted with an interior electric light bulb. The slightest movement would activate the spring, and the sealed box would fly open and release light and air into the coffin. At the same time a flag would extend outside the coffin, the interior light would switch itself on and a bell would ring for 30 minutes.

Modern-day embalmers Superglue the corpse's lips together to prevent the mouth from falling open.

While Cardinal Espinosa, the prime minister to Philip II of Spain, was being cut open in preparation for embalming, he sat up and grabbed the knife out the hand of the dissector before finally expiring.

The novelist Sir Walter Scott liked to break the ice at parties by introducing dinner guests to his novelty salt cellar, which was made from the fourth cervical vertebra of Charles I. The relic had been stolen by a surgeon during an autopsy on the royal corpse when Charles's long lost coffin was rediscovered at Windsor Castle in 1813. Scott kept it on his dining table for 30 years until Queen Victoria got to hear about it. She was distinctly unamused and ordered that it be returned to St George's chapel.

The average cost of a basic funeral in the UK in 1993 was £754. London's cheapest grave is in Hounslow (£230), its most expensive in Highgate (£2,200).

THE WISE AND THE GOOD

The 19th-century earl Lord Monboddo, reputed to be 'the most learned judge of his day', spent his life utterly convinced that babies were born with tails, and that there was a universal conspiracy of silence among midwives who cut them off at birth. Monboddo's conviction wasn't even swayed when he witnessed the births of his own children. He concluded that the crafty midwives had tricked him and destroyed the evidence.

In ancient Greece a slave's testimony in court wasn't considered reliable unless he had been tortured.

In the middle of an important criminal trial in 1977, Judge Alan King-Hamilton solemnly told the jury that 'the Australians are 4 for 1 wicket'. In 1986 Judge Michael Argyle told a jury that the lack of Test Match cricket on television was 'enough to make an Orthodox Jew want to join the Nazi party'.

Bestiality became a capital offence in Britain in the 16th century, but the law didn't see any difference between the human offender and the non-consenting animal. Burning at the stake was the recognised penalty for bestiality in 17th-century Scotland for both man and beast. On September 17th 1605 Johnne Jak was bound to a stake and burned alive, as was his favourite mare. In 1679 a woman and a dog hanged together on Tyburn Hill, London.

In 1972 the Los Angeles judge Justice Title awarded $4,500 damages to the owner of an elephant called Bimbo. The judge ruled that as a result of injuries received in a road accident, Bimbo had completely lost interest in dancing and water skiing.

The 18th-century British public thought that dissection for anatomical research was a well-earned penalty for murder, but there were still far too few dead criminals to go round. The 1752 English Act of Parliament to Prevent the Horrid Crime of Murder ruled that convicted murderers should be executed the day after sentence was passed (except on Sundays) and that at the discretion of the court their bodies should be given to surgeons for dissection and exhibition to the public. Thus the phrase 'your body shall be given to science' became part of the death sentence. Executed criminals were not allowed to receive a Christian burial, and were banned from even having the funeral service read to them on the way to the gallows. The aim was to reduce their hope of Salvation – and to ensure that their bodies were damningly dismembered and therefore unable to rise again on the Day of Judgement.

Ivan the Terrible's habit of rampaging through his home- land slaughtering thousands of peasants was aggravated by his tertiary syphilis, which produces bad-tempered and bellicose behaviour in the sufferer.

Raynor Goddard was one of the most enthusiastic hangers and floggers to have held the post of Lord Chief Justice. It is claimed that he was sexually aroused by sentencing young men to death, and achieved orgasm while pronouncing the death sentence. It was Goddard who sentenced 19-year-old Derek Bentley to hang in 1953, after Bentley had told his friend to 'let him have it, Chris'.

In 18th and early 19th-century Britain over 250 crimes carried the death penalty, including the theft of turnips and pickpocketing. As late as 1831 a boy aged nine was hanged at Chelmsford for arson. Women were occasion- ally spared hanging and burned instead for the sake of 'decency'.

In 1992 the Pennsylvanian judge Charles Guyer was sacked after a hidden video camera recorded him offer- ing a novel form of plea-bargaining. He offered convicted men lighter sentences if they allowed him to shampoo their hair.

In 1652 in Naples kissing in public became an offence punishable by death.

In 1983 a Manhattan criminal court judge was barred from office after deciding the length of a jail sentence on the toss of a coin, and asking courtroom spectators to vote on which of two conflicting witnesses was telling the truth.

One of the most bizarre court room exhibits of all time helped seal the fate of Charles Guiteau, the man who assassinated US President Garfield in 1881. The section of the President's spine which had been hit by Guiteau's bullet was produced in evidence and passed around the jury. When Guiteau was executed, ticket touts charged 250 spectators $300 a time to see him hanged.

For many senior judges showing off a complete ignorance of contemporary issues is all part of the job. In 1979, while presiding over a case involving the English Football Association, Mr Justice Cantley asked a barrister, 'Kevin Keegan, does he play for England or Scotland?' In 1985 Mr Justice Harman asked, 'Who is Bruce Springsteen?' Neither could compete with the Canadian judge who was completely baffled in 1977 by the occupation of one Keith Richard, on trial for possession of heroin. He asked Richard's defence counsel, 'Who are the Rolling Stones?'

The 17th-century judicial system was inclined to give ugly people a raw deal because ugliness was seen as a sure sign of guilt. The French legal expert Henri Boguet declared that the repulsiveness of a man's face was enough to expose him to torture to make him confess his crimes. Some European mediaeval laws decreed that whenever two people were under suspicion for the same crime, the better looking of the two was always the innocent one.

On 8 February 1986 a Philadelphia judge refused to convict a man for rape on the grounds that the alleged victim was 'the ugliest girl I have ever seen'. He went on to say that the experience had put him off rape trials for good and requested that he be excused from presiding over any more.

During the Holy Inquisition, animals were frequently tortured to extract 'confessions'. Their cries of pain were interpreted as confessions of guilt.

'The Boston Strangler' Albert de Salvo might have guessed that the game was up when his own trial defence counsel described him as 'a completely uncontrolled vegetable walking around in a human body'. De Salvo served only six years of his life sentence: another prisoner hacked him to death with a knife.

British prisons in the 18th century were so appallingly disease-ridden that in 1750 a group of prisoners from Newgate standing trial at the Old Bailey managed to infect the entire court room. Fifty people died, including the judge, jurors and spectators. In 1774 an Act of Parliament was passed to reduce the likelihood of 'jail fever' striking again, but it didn't mean cleaner jails. Prisoners were stripped of their clothes and forced to stand trial in carters' smocks. The British system of transporting criminals was originally designed to empty the notoriously insanitary jails. After the American Declaration of Independence in 1776, the British legal system was forced to find somewhere else to dump their convicts: up until that time it was to America, not Australia, that Britain sent most of her criminals.

Sir George 'Bloody' Jeffreys of Wem (1648–1689) was Britain's most sadistic Lord Chief Justice ever. He passed 331 death sentences and had hundreds more deported – usually a fate worse than hanging. One of his most notorious sentences was conferred on Lady Alice de Lisle, whom he ordered to be roasted alive. The Church was outraged by the sentence and demanded clemency: Lady Alice had her sentence commuted on appeal and got away with a beheading. Jeffreys didn't allow a word of self defence and always drove the prosecution through at high speed. The cause of this behaviour was his painful bladder-stone: he was compelled to urinate hourly and had to get through the trials as fast as possible to reach the lavatory.

Animals have been put on trial for committing crimes from biblical times until well into the 20th century. The trials were normally conducted along correct lines of legal practice and some lawyers established reputations as animal defence counsels. In 1471 a cockerel in Basle was found guilty by a Swiss court of laying an egg, and was condemned to death and burnt at the stake. In 1659 a gang of Italian caterpillars was summoned to appear in court to answer charges of trespass and wilful damage to property. The caterpillars failed to turn up to answer the charges, even though the authorities had taken the precaution of carefully nailing the summons to trees near the caterpillars' last known address. Pigs who broke the law in France were dressed in human clothing and publicly flogged. A sow was hanged in Normandy for killing and partially eating a child: her six accomplice piglets were also put on trial but acquitted, on account of their youth. In 1974 a dog in Libya was sentenced to a month's imprisonment for biting a man. In the 1930s in Cairo two performing monkeys, accused of being accomplices to a pickpocket, were put to death by firing squad.

The longest serving prisoner in Broadmoor's history was Bill Giles, who died in prison in 1962 aged 87. He was committed at the age of 11 for setting fire to a hayrick.

IMMORAL, ILLEGAL AND FATTENING

Genghis Khan, whose conquests covered most of the known world, whipped his men into a frenzy before a battle by getting them high on hashish.

About 4,000 different plants can, in some form or other, be used as mind-altering drugs. You can actually get high on nutmeg, but you will need to take at least 20 grams to do it.

The great Chief Sitting Bull was regularly stoned on cannabis and wrote detailed accounts of his experiences while under the influence. It may have been the Sioux nation's fondness for pot that ensured the slaughter to the last man of Custer and his 7th Cavalry, at the Battle of the Little Big Horn. The Indians were incensed because Custer's troops had unwittingly trampled through an area where the sacred herb was grown.

In the 1970s Elvis's kitchen was manned 24 hours a day, but the busiest time was around 4.30 a.m. when the King liked to binge on three huge cheeseburgers and six or seven banana splits. As he was usually heavily drugged by this time with a massive concoction of barbiturates and tranquilisers, Elvis's aides frequently had to save him from choking to death by reaching down his throat to remove food lodged in his windpipe.

The British Prime Minister George Canning was addicted to laudanum, an hallucinatory drug derived from opium.

Sir Walter Raleigh was a dedicated pipe smoker who, if he hadn't had his head chopped off, may have become Europe's first lung cancer statistic.

Lord Liverpool, British Prime Minister from 1812 to 1827 was addicted to ether.

Pot was often grown freely by American 18th-century plantation owners and the landed gentry, and smoked for pleasure. George Washington's diary of 1765 records that he grew and smoked his own cannabis and, unlike Bill Clinton, knew that there wasn't much point to it unless you inhaled.

Depending on which official Church explanation you believed, the Black Death was caused by wearing winklepicker shoes, going to the theatre or hanging around with witches.

Prader-Willi syndrome is a rare brain disorder which condemns the victim to a lifetime's constant craving for food. Sufferers often become so obese that they suffocate in their own flab.

Elvis's favourite reading matter, apart from the Bible, was the Physician's Desk Reference. During the last two and a half years of his life, Elvis received more than 19,000 doses of narcotics, stimulants, sedatives and anti-depressants from his personal physician alone. Dr George Nichopoulos was tried and convicted in 1981 for overprescribing drugs, but as Elvis had dozens of other secret sources, including dentists, the full picture of his drug abuse will never be known. The pathologist who compiled the toxicology report on Presley after his death in 1977 testified that he had never seen so many drugs in one body.

Before it was finally banned in 1906 the use of cocaine was widespread. Shops freely sold cocaine bonbons, cocaine cigarettes, even cocaine ointment. Sigmund Freud endorsed cocaine as a 'stimulating euphorant'. The popularity of Coca Cola was helped by the fact that many people believed that the soft drink contained a large shot of the drug.

William Wilberforce, the philanthropist who ensured the abolition of the slave trade, was an opium addict.

In pre-war Nazi Germany cocaine was hugely popular with the rich and powerful – the head of the Luftwaffe

Hermann Goering was a notorious cocaine and morphine addict. Some historians have made a connection between the delusions of strength and paranoia suffered by cocaine abusers and similar traits displayed by Nazi leaders: it has even been speculated that Hitler may have been on a cocaine trip when he decided to conquer Russia.

The poet and dramatist W. B. Yeats took mescaline, a powerful hallucinogenic drug derived from a Mexican cactus.

In the 17th century smokers were tortured in Russia and executed in Germany.

The fattest person in medical history was Jon Brower of Washington State, USA. He peaked at 99 stone 1lb, but by the time of his death in 1982 had wasted to a sleek 57 stone.

Sigmund Freud continued to choke his way through 20 large cigars a day even after doctors told him he had cancer of the mouth.

The first British Prime Minister Sir Robert Walpole swallowed about 180lb of soap in the last few years of his life in an attempt to get rid of a stone in his bladder.

In 1992 the Englishman John McGuire was found to have swallowed a record-breaking 58 condoms in an attempt to smuggle half a pound of cannabis resin into

Australia. They were discovered after he was admitted to hospital with a suspected burst appendix.

Cocaine snorters often find that their habit has rotted away the membranes separating their nasal passages. Status Quo's Francis Rossi claimed that after several years of cocaine abuse his favourite party trick to dissuade young people from taking the drug was to pass a handkerchief up one nostril and then down the other.

The comatose Soviet leader Leonid Brezhnev spent the last ten years of his life as a tranquiliser and sleeping pill junkie. His prolific drug abuse accelerated the ageing process and caused massive damage to his central nervous system. Brezhnev's public appearances were so famous for their lack of animation that they inspired widespread rumours that he was always long dead. His assistants later admitted that during a state visit to East Germany in 1979 they had to set the drugged President on his feet and propel him forward as though they were 'kick-starting a car'.

Charles Dickens took opium: Samuel Coleridge became addicted to it.

Keith Richards's appetite for recreational substances was more than equalled by the former Rolling Stone Brian Jones, but the latter didn't have the metabolism to go with it. Jones was once described as 'the most beautiful man in London', but his abuse of drugs and alcohol bequeathed him, at the age of 29, the vital organs of a geriatric. After Jones was found dead at the bottom of his swimming pool on 2 July 1969, a few weeks after being fired by his band, the pathologist reported that his heart was abnormally large, and his liver twice the normal weight and in an advanced stage of fatty degeneration.

In the 19th century boxers regularly used heroin for its anaesthetic and stimulating properties. Many of the apparently 'punch-drunk' boxers were in fact displaying obvious signs of heroin addiction. A popular method used by trainers to keep a fighter alert while he was high on heroin was to run a naked flame down his back.

In large enough doses, caffeine can be used by athletes as a performance boosting drug. Tests on urine samples at the Seoul Olympics showed that some athletes had dosed themselves with caffeine through the rectum by the use of caffeine-laced suppositories.

The French poet Charles Baudelaire died insane, paralysed and speechless in 1867 at the age of 46 as a result of his syphilis and addiction to drink, hashish and opium.

Elvis Presley was addicted to Freenamint laxative chewing gum, but it didn't do much for him: he died falling off his toilet seat with a heart attack while straining to overcome constipation.

Over an eight-month period in 1992, refuse collectors on the New York subway collected four tons of syringes discarded by drug addicts.

The world's most extensively used mind-altering drug is caffeine, although it is almost impossible to take a fatal overdose of it unless you're capable of drinking about 300 cups of coffee in under 15 minutes.

Thomas de Quincey, the author of *Confessions of an Opium Eater*, degenerated into a physically repulsive wreck thanks to his habit of quaffing up to 8,000 drops of opium and six or seven glasses of laudanum a day. His skin took on the complexion of cracked parchment and he lost most of his teeth. He also had a habit of setting fire to his hair while poring over his manuscripts by candlelight.

The novelist Arnold Bennett died of typhoid in 1931 after drinking a glass of Paris tapwater to show everybody how safe it was.

Japanese servicemen were regularly given amphetamines during World War II to keep them awake. In less than ten years the number of known amphetamine addicts in Japan rose from a few to more than 200,000.

Arthur Conan Doyle was a cocaine user, and had his most famous character Sherlock Holmes use it in his story 'The Sign of Four'.

Although opium is one of the most toxic plant poisons on earth, it was widely used in patent medicines, especially cough mixtures, in the early 1900s. In a five year period 1,500 people in England and Wales died as a result of taking opium-based patent medicines.

Robert Louis Stevenson's *Dr Jekyll and Mr Hyde* was entirely cocaine-induced. He snorted vast quantities of the drug while working on it, which was why he was able to write and twice revise the 60,000 word manuscript inside six days.

Eskimo is the world's only culture completely devoid of mind-altering chemical substances.

50 ways to leave your liver
Jack Mytton, the wealthy 19th-century MP and squire of Halston in Shropshire, squandered an inheritance of around £500,000 thanks largely to an incredible capacity for alcohol, and eventually died a bloated, paralysed and penniless debtor in the King's Bench prison. Mytton reputedly got through eight bottles of brandy and eight bottles of port every day. After his death in 1834 at the age of 38, a friend signed an affidavit to the effect that

Mytton had been permanently pissed for the last twelve years of his life. His death was partly attributed to injuries sustained while setting fire to his own night-shirt to try to cure hiccups. Just before the horribly burned Mytton slumped into unconsciousness he said, 'Well, the hiccups is gone, by God.'

The Goths of ancient Germany had a custom of debating all important state matters twice – once sober, and once drunk.

Pitt the Younger was a prolific port drinker who often made speeches in the House of Commons when drunk. Before making important interventions in debates Pitt went behind the Speaker's Chair to throw up.

Alexander the Great, the bisexual Macedonian king who ruled an empire stretching from Greece to India, was a chronic alcoholic famed just as much for his marathon drinking sessions as for his military conquests. During one of Alexander's drinking contests 35 men died. During another bout he killed one of his closest friends with a spear. Alexander finally dropped dead during a drinking contest at the age of 32. His friend Hephaestion expired while drinking half a gallon of wine for breakfast.

Winston Churchill was soused through most of World War II: his drinking sessions usually started late in the morning and went on until the early hours.

Although Britain has some of the strictest licensing laws

in Europe, the bars of the House of Commons are and always have been exempt.

When the USA Congress introduced Total Prohibition in 1919, the American medical profession recommended morphine as an ideal substitute for alcohol. During Prohibition about 35,000 Americans were killed by drinking moonshine and other forms of illegal liquor.

Selim II, Sultan of the Ottomans from 1566 to 1574, could drink a bottle of Cyprus wine without drawing breath. When he ran out of his favourite tipple and one of his advisers suggested he capture Cyprus, the mad Turkish leader eagerly agreed. His men massacred 30,000 Cypriot Christians in the process, and their leader Bragadino was flayed alive and his skin stuffed with straw and displayed to the Turkish troops.

W. C. Fields was quite happy to be Hollywood's best known alcoholic and drank two quarts of martini a day. Whenever he travelled, he took three trunks with him: one for his clothes and two for his liquid refreshment.

Alice Cooper (*né* Vincent Furnier) is rock and roll's greatest surviving dipsomaniac. He went on the wagon after committing himself to a sanatorium in 1977 when his intake reached two quarts of whisky and up to 40 cans of beer a day. His band at that time were spending £150,000 a year on booze.

Guinness dropped pint-swallowing from their *Book of*

Records in 1971, because the activities of people swilling up to 65 pints of beer an hour by regurgitating every fourth or fifth pint were not very good for the company image. The last record entry was that of Horst Pretorius of West Germany, who knocked back just under 40 pints of beer in one hour and kept it all down.

The Bourbon kings of France were famous for their gluttony. Louis XIV could stuff away vast quantities of food and wine well into his eighties – his incredible appetite even in old age fed a widespread rumour that the king was inhabited by a giant tapeworm. His appetite abated only when he began a lingering and agonising death through gangrene, which began when his left leg turned black and began to stink. Louis XVI had to be carried to bed most evenings after gorging himself senseless, and was widely referred to by his courtiers simply as 'the fat pig'. The obese Louis XVIII inherited the Bourbon appetite, but suffered from a variety of ailments, including gout and dropsy, which transformed him in old age to a living skeleton. By 1823 he was in such a state of physical decay that one evening, when his valets were removing the king's sock, they found a loose toe.

THE JOY OF SEX

Attila the Hun, despite being very short, squat and plug ugly, had twelve wives. He died when he burst an artery while bedding a beautiful virgin.

In 1981 French magistrates gave an 80-year-old prostitute a 10-month suspended prison sentence. The Paris court heard that Madame Marie Louise Soccodato had been plying her trade since 1941, although lately business had been dropping off.

The original sheath was invented by a London surgeon, Mr Condom in around 1750. It was made from lamb gut. The intestines were washed and dried, then made supple by rolling them between the palms of the hands with bran and olive oil. There is no record of a Mrs Femidom.

A 72-year-old doctor caused a sensation in 1889 when he gave a lecture to the French Society of Biology about how he had discovered the elixir of youth. Dr Charles Brown-Séquard described how he chopped and ground up the testicles of puppies and guinea pigs, then injected himself with the resulting compound. He announced that he was now physically thirty years younger and boasted that he was able to 'visit' his young wife every day without fail. The lecture caused a stir in the medical establishment, albeit briefly: soon afterwards his wife left him for a younger man, and shortly after that the doctor dropped dead from a cerebral haemorrhage.

Catherine the Great of Russia was both an insomniac and a nymphomaniac, which was very bad news for the dozens of handsome young soldiers she continued to bed well into her seventies. She advocated sexual intercourse six times a day, had 21 'official' lovers, and employed a doctor to examine all new applicants.

The Russian surgeon Serge Voronoff started to study Egyptian court eunuchs when it occurred to him that most of them looked remarkably good for their age, and concluded that male sex glands rejuvenated the body. In 1920 he put his theories to the test: he took the testicles of a chimpanzee and grafted them onto a 73-year-old man. Voronoff recorded that his experiment only had 'a temporary effect'.

Adolph Hitler's mistress Eva Braun confided to friends that their famous affair was completely sexless. Apart from the Führer's syphilis, he'd also apparently experienced a boyhood mishap with a wild alpine goat which left him with permanently damaged testicles.

The famous prude George Bernard Shaw finally lost his virginity, to an elderly widow, at the age of 29. He was

moved by the experience so much that he didn't bother
to try it again for another 15 years.

Love hurts

King Louis XVI didn't consummate his marriage with
Marie Antionette until nearly seven years after their
wedding day because of a freak disorder of the royal
penis. Louis suffered from an abnormally overgrown
foreskin – a major drawback which made erections
painful and sex completely out of the question. He
reluctantly agreed to undergo corrective surgery, and
lost his virginity on his 23rd birthday.

The US Patents Office currently holds plans for five
anti-rape devices designed to horribly mutilate the
assailant. In 1977 inventor Charles Barlow of Arizona
patented a device designed to be inserted into a woman's
vagina. It contained three spears with harpoon-like
barbs which would embed themselves into the penis of
the would-be rapist. Anna Pennystone's anti-rape device, patented in 1983, also involved a rigid sheath
inserted into the woman: the inside of the device was
coated with adhesive and contained a pouch of chemicals
which would burn the flesh. Others included Alston
Levasque's 'Penis Locking and Lacerating Vaginal Insert', and George Vogel's 'Female Protective Device' – a
large lump of metal with a solid spear in the centre. A
creation devised by Joel Rumph and Lynda Warren,
meanwhile, offers to inject the assailant's penis with a
fast-working sedative thus rendering him unconscious.
None of them ever got off the drawing board largely

because of a basic design flaw – each device would have to be big enough to house an erect penis and would make wearing them extremely uncomfortable, not to mention highly dangerous if any of them went off spontaneously.

After sex, the female marine bristleworm eats her partner's sex organ.

The Romanian King Carol II had such a gargantuan appetite for sex that he had to create the full-time job of official court abortionist to keep pace with his hobby. King Carol reputedly slept with thousands of women, and was said to have had such an abnormally huge penis that intercourse killed several of his mistresses.

The most expensive one-night stand in history took place in 1850. The prostitute and part-time evangelist Laura Bell, who lived in Grosvenor Square, London, reputedly charged Prince Jung Badahur, Prime Minister of Nepal, £250,000 for services rendered.

You've Lost that Lovin' Feeling
In central Europe until the late 18th century, if a betrothed girl died before the marriage the prospective bridegroom was expected to consummate the marriage by having intercourse with the corpse. A similar custom existed in Burma and parts of India.

The supposition that professional sportsmen, especially boxers, should avoid sex before a contest because it might sap their strength has a long tradition. In ancient Greece top athletes were prevented from having intercourse by having their foreskins tied up.

James Dean's pubic lice gave him so much trouble while he was making 'Rebel Without A Cause' that the film's director had to drag him away to a chemist's to find a lotion. He constantly scratched at his genitals on the film set much to the embarrassment of his co-star Natalie Wood.

The queen bee has sex only once in a lifetime, an arrangement the male bee can happily live with. When his job is done his organ snaps off inside her as a plug to prevent sperm leakage. He then bleeds to death. At least he dies happy: the Queen's unsuccessful suitors return to the hive to die of starvation.

Mohandas 'Mahatma' Gandhi slept with several young women at a time. He said it gave him strength during his long fasts.

Pubic lice – *'papillons d'amour'* to the French and 'crabs' to the English – are passed through sexual intercourse but don't live exclusively in pubic hair: they also like taking up residence in beards and eyelashes.

You can go off people, you know . . .
Two of the most popular anaphrodisiacs in mediaeval times were pigeon dung and snail excrement. It was also

widely believed throughout Europe that a man hopelessly in love with a woman could suppress his sexual urges by placing some of her excrement in his shoe and wearing it.

For the lucky male giraffe foreplay involves drinking the female's urine to find out whether or not she will be receptive to his advances.

The 18th-century manual *Grimorium Verum* advised the following as a useful aphrodisiac: 'Go to a stews (public baths) and stay in the hottest part of it until you are sweating profusely. Dust yourself with sufficient white flour to absorb fully the sweat and then brush off the flour into a bag and take it home with you. Place the flour into a bowl, add to it clippings from your nails (finely chopped of course), and add a few hairs from both the scalp and pubic area. Then make a cake mixture from your favourite recipe and add the previously compounded unpleasantness to it before baking. Serve it to your intended lover or mistress, who will then find your approaches irresistible.'

Until the 18th century, Germans believed that menstrual blood was an aphrodisiac: women would mix some of their menstrual blood into their husband's food and drink.

Lord Palmerston was probably Britain's randiest ever Prime Minister – a prolific womaniser to the end of his days. He had affairs with three well-known society hostesses of the day – if a Commons debate clashed with a party, the debate was postponed. He was accused by Queen Victoria of attempting to rape one of her ladies-in-waiting during a visit to Windsor Castle, and in 1862 was cited as co-respondent in a divorce at the age of 78. Palmerston continued to make passes at married women into his eighties while still Prime Minister.

The French President Francois Faure (1841–1899) died on the job with a whore in a brothel. Faure's death sent the woman into shock and his member had to be surgically removed from her.

In the Middle Ages the Christian church grudgingly admitted that sex was necessary, but drew the line at enjoying it: they decreed that any pleasure derived from sexual intercourse was the devil's work and contact with the female body should therefore be reduced to the absolute minimum. The most extreme result of this was the passion-killing *chemise cagoule* – an armour-plated nightie with a stategically placed hole.

Tonight's the night

Stentor coeruleus is a primitive organism capable of reproducing without coupling, but once a year the male and female enjoy a 36-hour orgy which kills them both.

Sarah Bernhardt, said to have been France's finest actress, had more than 1,000 lovers but only one leg.

The highly esteemed 19th-century Tory Cabinet minister and churchman Lewis Harcourt made himself unpopular with Reginald, the 2nd Viscount of Esher, by first trying to sodomise his son and later by trying to rape his daughter. Harcourt finally committed suicide after the mother of a 12-year-old boy he'd tried to rape spilled the beans. Harcourt's death was rewritten in The Complete Peerage *as death by heart failure in his sleep.*

For many species of male spiders sex is a deadly business. During or shortly after intercourse the female mantis spider bites off her lover's head then eats the rest of his body. The male's sex drive is so strong he continues on the job even while he is being eaten alive. Some female crickets have a similarly abrupt post-coital manner. The female scorpion takes part in a touching courtship ritual, but as soon as fertilisation is successful she makes a meal of her partner. The male wheel-web spider usually dies of exhaustion and starvation after a marathon sex session, then the female immediately leaps on his body and eats him. The female ant lion not only eats her partner after sex, but also any other passing male ant she can catch. More wily male partners resort to bondage before sex to ensure they escape with their lives. Some tropical spiders offer their intended a pleasant-tasting secretion, taken from a gland in the thorax – a desperate tactic to prevent the female from killing him during copulation. The idea is that she is less likely to eat him if her mouth is already full.

The sex-mad monk Rasputin (the name is Russian for 'debauchee') was leader of a pseudo-religious cult called Khlysky, which carried out orgies of bloody self-mutilation followed by mass copulation. Rasputin is said to have bedded every female aristocrat in St Petersburg more than once, even though he smelled like an open sewer. He didn't believe in bathing and often went for months without washing his hands or face, offering the excuse that water sapped his libido. His body odour was so bad that women bathed themselves in perfume before sleeping with him to try to overpower it.

The mouse-like marsupial called the swamp antechinus copulates so enthusiastically that it usually drops dead afterwards from exhaustion or starvation.

Pope Gregory XI frequently complained about the number of illegitimate children born to nuns from liaisons with priests and monks. In the late 14th century many of the convents were little more than brothels.

Pope Leo VIII died of a heart attack while having sex.

If the cap fits . . .
Ancient Egyptian women made their own pessaries from
crocodile dung.

Until the 19th century, coitus interruptus, infanticide,
and alcohol-soaked sponges were the most popular
means of birth control. Other methods to control population included polyandry and the forcing of people into
homosexual relationships. An Aboriginal tribe in the
19th century killed one child born in every ten so that
the population wouldn't exceed the territory they
inhabited.

The personal brothel of Louis XV was said to have been
the biggest ever to accommodate the needs of one man.
Set in the grounds of his palace at Versailles, it employed a huge staff and cost £200,000 a year to maintain.
The king's procurers were expected to make a constant
supply of girls aged between nine and eighteen available
for the royal bed, although it was only during the last
three years that they were obliged to be in 'active
service'. When the girls outstayed their welcome by
reaching the ripe old age of nineteen they were either
married off or despatched to a convent. Over a period of
34 years a steady stream of girls passed through Louis's
brothel, and there was apparently no shortage of volunteers. Families considered that a few years of shame

was a price well worth paying for the guarantee of lifelong security for their daughters thereafter.

Nymphomania was believed in the Far East to be the result of worms in the vagina.

When the female bumblebee eelworm mates it always results in the death of the male. The female doesn't get off lightly either: she then undergoes an incredible transformation, as her sex organ inflates until it is 20,000 times bigger than she is. Her body then withers away and dies.

London's Coppice Alley and Grape Street, both formerly famous for prostitution, were originally called Codpiece Alley and Gropecunt Lane.

Size matters . . .

More than 40,000 penis implant operations are performed annually in the US, but not all are successful. One of the most regular side-effects is Pyronees Disease, which results in a permanently bent penis. Cosmetic surgeons in Miami offer penis enlargement operations for as little as £1,300. Augmentation phalloplasty will lengthen the penis by up to 1.5 inches;

circumferential autologous penile enlargement makes it thicker.

Ancient Egyptian men rubbed crocodile dung into their phalluses to make them bigger.

Arabs developed their own method of penis enlargement which involve the application of hot pitch, leeches and boiled asses' private parts.

To celebrate the 57th birthday of King Bhumibol of Thailand on 8 March 1985, 1,200 loyal subjects had vasectomies performed upon them by a team of 60 doctors doing one vasectomy every two minutes.

Columbus, Ferdinand Magellan and Captain Cook all had syphilis, as did Beethoven, Gauguin, Goethe, Schumann, John Keats, Freidrich Nietzsche, the Marquis de Sade, General Custer and Al Capone.

What's this crazy little thing called, love?
The Dayak tribe of Borneo decorate their phalluses by inserting metal rods through them with golden balls at each end.

Aboriginal tribesmen in Australia occasionally slit their penises open to imitate the forked penis of the kangaroo.

The greatest known age difference between a married couple is 88 years. In Bangladesh in 1983, 16-year-old Marium Begun became the fifth wife of 104-year-old Amin Ali Azam.

At the turn of the century the rate of VD infection was so great in the British Army in India – around 50% – that General Kitchener issued a memorandum to his troops to try to stop them from sleeping with Indian women. Venereal disease, explained Kitchener, 'assumes a horrible loathsome form . . . the sufferer finds his hair falling off, the skin and the flesh of his body rot, and are eaten away by slow cancerous ulcerations, his nose falls off, and he eventually becomes blind: his throat is eaten away by foetid ulcerations which cause his breath to stink'. There was little danger of the great general himself being tempted by the local whores: Kitchener shared a bed with his male military secretary.

In 1987 Japan's Nippon TV station reported that an actress Hitoko Tagawa had volunteered to have sex with an ape called Oliver 'in the interests of research'. Oliver's owner was so taken by her offer he filed a £750,000 lawsuit against the TV station.

Frederick the Great never consummated his marriage to the Princess Elizabeth. It was widely believed that as a young man he had suffered such a dire bout of venereal disease that the only cure was castration.

Some African tribes developed a drastic method of ensuring that only the chief's eldest son could procreate. All of the chief's younger sons were cut transversely across the urethra, thereby ensuring impotence.

HONEY, I ATE THE KIDS

The Carib Indians, first discovered by Columbus when he was shipwrecked in the West Indies, were the cannibal world connoisseurs of human *haute cuisine*. (The local dialect of the word 'Carib' is *Caniba* – the origin of the word cannibal.) Caribs even bred children expressly for edible purposes: the children were first castrated because it improved the flavour. Columbus noted that the Caribs considered the French to be the very tastiest people in the world.

In 1945 a German soldier who had been accidently left behind in the German retreat was discovered by the Allies locked in an abandoned railroad truck in Belgium. He had survived by eating portions of his left leg and drinking his own blood.

Captain James Cook, who had often written in his journals about the cannibalistic habits of Fijiian, Samoan and New Zealand tribesmen, probably ended up as an Hawaiian buffet. All that Cook's men could find of him after he had been killed and dismembered at a

heianu ceremony at Keala Kekua were a few bones and
some salted flesh.

A man weighing 150lb (68kg) would provide enough
meat to provide a meal for 75 cannibals in one sitting.

Throughout the great Egyptian famine of 1201, many
survived by slaughtering and eating children. A Cairo
doctor named Abdi al-Latif left a detailed diary of the
famine. Children were regularly kidnapped only to end
up on someone's dining table and were often sold
ready-roasted or boiled. Latif described how a woman
was caught red-handed and was dragged before the
authorities with a roasted child still hanging around her
neck. Grave-robbers even ate, and sold, the bodies they
dug up. People who had been caught eating human flesh
often tried to excuse themselves by claiming that they
were only eating the remains of a close relative. At first
the authorities made a determined effort to stamp out
the practice by burning the culprits, but in time the
Egyptians grew indifferent to cannibalism. The mania
for eating children eventually spread to the rich, by
which time it had become a fashion, rather than a
necessity. Often two or three children at a time were
thrown into a single cook-pot: on one occasion the
authorities found ten assorted heads marinating in a
selection of choice herbs and spices.

Bottoms up . . .

The cannibal Cubeo tribe of Brazil was skilled in creating the world's most grisly cocktail: they exhumed a partially cremated corpse, burned the bones to ashes, mixed it with the local brew then drank it.

America's most bizarre mail order con began in 1946 and lasted for a decade. With rumours circulating that Adolf Hitler had been smuggled out of Germany after World War II and was alive and well, a semi-literate miner called William Johnson posed as Hitler, claiming that he had settled in Kentucky with some of his Nazi chiefs-of-staff and was plotting to take over the USA. He tricked money out of mostly right wing Americans and German emigrées by letting them in on his secret plans for space ships, invisible ships and underground hordes of ammunition. The fact that he often signed his name as The Furrier instead of the Führer didn't stop them from sending him a flood of postal orders worth tens of thousands of dollars.

When the Chinese famine of 206 BC killed half the population, human flesh became the staple diet. The taste for human flesh however seems to have lingered on long after the famine. During the T'ang dynasty in the late 9th and 10th centuries cannibalism was permitted by law and human flesh was sold publicly in street markets.

Grandfather Albert Fish went to the electric chair at Sing Sing prison in 1936 after killing and eating at least 15 children. His final victim was a 10-year-old girl. Fish wrote to the mother six years after she'd vanished: 'Grace sat on my lap and kissed me. I made up my mind to eat her.'

Neanderthal man was probably a cannibal by instinct. Many prehistoric skulls discovered with their bottoms bashed out may have indicated a quick way of turning a skull into a drinking vessel, but the more likely explanation was that it was done to eat out the brains. Archaeologists say that the unusually large number of cracked skulls and broken bones at Stone Age sites point to the fact that our ancestors were quite partial to human brain and loved to suck on a bit of juicy bone marrow whenever it was available.

African tribesmen captured and sold for slavery in the 18th century believed that their white captors were cannibals, and that white men bought negroes for the purpose of either eating them themselves or selling them to be eaten by others. They could imagine no other reason for their capture.

Sole food

Marco Polo noted in 1275 that the people of south east Asia ate the feet of their captives, believing them to be 'the most savoury food in the world'.

Red Indian tribes in Canada and around New York forced prisoners to swallow pieces of their own flesh.

In 1854 a single child's nappy killed 616 people in Soho, London. The outbreak of Asiatic Cholera took its toll after water used to wash the infected nappy entered the public drinking supply from a leaking cesspool in Broad Street.

The cannibal Tartar hordes who swept over Europe in 1242 were particularly fond of girls. Appetising young maidens were issued as rations to army officers, while common soldiers chewed on the tough flesh of older women. Breast meat was regarded as the finest titbit, and was reserved for the prince's table.

Police raiding the apartment of the Milwaukee cannibal Jeffrey Dahmer found severed heads in the fridge, skulls in his filing cabinet and body parts in a kettle. When they found a human heart in the deep freeze, Dahmer explained, 'I was saving it for later.'

The enemy within

In the 1890s French soldiers fighting in Tonkin risked becoming a Chinese take-away. Oriental soldiers ate their enemies in the belief that human flesh, especially foreign flesh, was a great stimulant for a man's courage.

The idea that you could acquire the bravery and other desirable qualities of your enemy by eating him has a long history. Maori cannibals did most of their dining *al fresco* on the battlefield and even carried portable steam ovens with them so they could butcher and eat their enemies on the spot. The cannibal Apiaca tribe of Brazil, who were still having people for dinner as late as 1848, roasted and ate the bodies of enemies taken in battle. A captured child of an enemy would be raised by an Apiaca family as their own, until the age of twelve to fourteen, when the foster father would creep up behind the child and bash his or her skull in. The children were then eaten during all-night feasts.

The Sioux Chief Rain In The Face admitted that after the Battle of the Little Big Horn in 1877 he had cut out the heart of General Custer and eaten a slice of it. He said he didn't much like the taste of human flesh – he just wanted to get his own back.

Some Japanese troops during World War II are known to have eaten their prisoners-of-war.

In the Ukrainian and Russian famines of the 1920s peasants openly resorted to cannibalism. According to Kruschev's memoirs, one of his men reported that in

1947 a woman half-demented with hunger had dismembered and eaten her own children.

A Man for All Seasonings

The anthropologist Paul Shankman once compiled a world-wide cannibal cook book which listed the various ways mankind has chosen to cook his fellow man. It includes pot-boiling, spit-roasting, steam-baking, cooking on pre-heated rocks, in earth ovens, smoking, drying, powdering, stuffing, and eating raw. The most unsavoury preparation in Shankman's menu involved burying the body, then exhuming it and eating the putrefying flesh. The maggots were scraped off, wrapped in banana leaves, and eaten separately as an entrée.

During the retreat of Napoleon's Grand Army from Moscow, dead soldiers were eaten both by their French comrades and by scavenging Russian peasants. A similar fate befell the corpses of some British soldiers in the disastrous retreat from Kabul in 1842 during the First Afghan War.

Ed Gein, a middle-aged cannibal from Wisconsin, was the inspiration for the film *Psycho* and later *Silence of the Lambs*. Gein started by digging up female corpses to satisfy his perversion and graduated to murder as a means of obtaining bodies. A police raid on Gein's well-stocked fridge in 1957 helped account for 15 bodies. They found human-skin bracelets, a human drum-skin, two lips on a string, four noses in a cup and dozens of human organs. Gein later admitted that he enjoyed draping himself in the skin of his dead victims.

The Bindewars of India and Central Asia regularly ate their sick and elderly in the belief that it would appease Kali, the goddess of plagues, epidemics and cholera.

During the Allied blockade on Germany during World War I, Germans routinely used human flesh as sausage meat.

The most prolific homicidal cannibal of all was Fritz Haarmann, a dealer of meat in Germany shortly after World War I. Haarmann picked up mostly young male refugees at a railway station. After luring them back to his home by offering them food and shelter, he killed them and sold the flesh for meat, eating what he couldn't sell. It was estimated that Haarmann averaged two victims per week. He was only ever charged with 27 murders, although records show that in one year alone over 600 youths had disappeared in his native Hanover.

FAMILIA HORRIBILIS

William I abolished capital punishment in England, but his motives weren't entirely charitable: he preferred to castrate, mutilate and blind people instead so that they were walking advertisements to his authority.

Henry I, who fathered at least 21 illegitimate children, died from eating 'a surfeit of lampreys'.

Henry II kept a court jester named Roland who was required to fart for the amusement of his guests at the annual Christmas Day banquet.

Richard I spent less than three years of his entire reign in England, and during the Third Crusade indulged in cannibalism: he once dined on curried head of Saracen.

Edward II had a series of wild homosexual flings, including a scandalous affair with Piers Gaveston. Later he took a father and son to his bed, Messrs Hugh Despenser Sr and Jr, thus incurring the wrath of his wife. Queen Isabella had all three of Edward's lovers hanged, but had something altogether more interesting in mind for her husband. She arranged for him to be incarcerated in Berkeley Castle, then had him assassinated first by suffocation and then by the application of a red-hot poker thrust up his rectum.

When Henry V died of dysentery just outside Paris his body was boiled in a cauldron and dismembered before it was shipped home. His cask was filled with incense – a wise precaution because it was two months before he could be interred.

Henry VI suffered from mental illness for much of his reign, possibly a legacy from his lunatic grandfather Charles VI of France. In 1453 he had a complete mental breakdown which lasted seventeen months, during which time he couldn't recognise his own wife.

Edward IV was a compulsive eater and drinker who grew grossly obese. He liked to force himself to vomit between courses so that he could gorge on more food.

Richard III allegedly had his own brother, the Duke of Clarence, drowned in a barrel of wine. Richard is the only English king since the Battle of Hastings to have no known grave. During the dissolution of the monasteries, his grave was rifled and his remains tossed into the River Soar at Leicester. His coffin was used as a horse trough.

Henry VII's most cherished souvenir was St George's left leg.

Due to an unfortunate oversight Henry VII's wife Queen Katherine lay above ground, neglected and covered only by a loose cloth in an open wooden cask, for several hundred years in Westminster Abbey for all to see. Samuel Pepys had a birthday treat when he went to visit the corpse on 23 February 1668. 'I had the upper part of her body in my hands, and I did kiss her mouth, reflecting upon it that I did kiss a Queene, and this was my birthday.' By the time Pepys stole his kiss she had been dead for over 230 years.

The British National Anthem was originally written as 'Dieu Sauvez le Roi' by French nuns at the cloister of Saint-Cyr to celebrate King Louis XIV's successful recovery from an operation on his anal fistulas.

Henry VIII's syphilis may have been the reason behind his difficulty in siring an heir, and his bad-tempered behaviour. During his 38-year reign he had about 72,000 people put to death.

Anne Boleyn had a distressing habit, first observed during her coronation banquet, of vomiting during meals. She employed a lady-in-waiting whose job it was to hold up a sheet when the Queen looked likely to throw up.

If Henry VIII's charges against Anne Boleyn of adultery and incest hadn't stuck, he planned to have her burnt as a witch because she had twelve fingers and three breasts.

Henry VIII's sickly son, Edward VI, reigned for just six years. His death at fifteen was officially explained as consumption, or more correctly tuberculosis. The symptoms, however, fitted the pattern of syphilis, not TB: he died bald and without fingernails. Mary Tudor also had syphilis, as did Elizabeth I, Mary Queen of Scots and James II.

Elizabeth I 'swore like a man' – a trait she inherited from her father Henry VIII, who was famous for his foul language. In her later years it was widely rumoured around her court that she had grown a beard.

Elizabeth I boasted that she had a bath once a month 'whether she need it or no'.

When Elizabeth I died of pneumonia she lay in state for several weeks and her coffin was watched over at night by relays of ladies-in-waiting. Elizabeth had left orders that she was not to be disembowelled or embalmed, and gradual decomposition would have led to a build-up of gases in her body. According to an eye-witness, Elizabeth Southwell, Elizabeth's body burst open one night 'with such a crack that it slit the coffin open'.

James I, who once said of Parliament, 'I am surprised that my ancestors should have allowed such an institution to come into existence', was very small, bisexual, never washed, had a speech impediment as a result of an abnormally large tongue, and an unfortunate habit of scratching his genitals in public. He died of dysentery.

Charles II was the first person ever to use a condom.

When Charles II and his court spent the summer of 1665 in Oxford to escape the Plague, the locals were outraged by their 'rude' behaviour, and noted that 'at their departure their excrement was left in every corner, in chimneys, coalhouses and cellars'. Charles died after having a fit while shaving.

The deposed Stuart king James II had his body buried at the priory church of the English Benedectine monks in Paris, his head and brains deposited in the Scots College, Paris, and most of his bowels buried at the parish church of St Germain.

The hook-nosed King William III was a well-known bisexual: his wife Mary may also have been bisexual. They died heirless.

Queen Anne had lesbian relationships with the Duchess of Marlborough, Sarah Jennings and the Duchess's cousin and royal bedchamber maid, Abigail Hill.

Queen Anne and her husband Prince George of Denmark were alcoholics.

Queen Anne also suffered from gout, and although she was very short she was so bloated she had to be carried throughout her coronation in a large chair.

All of Queen Anne's seventeen children died before she did. Only one, William, Duke of Gloucester, made it through infancy. He expired at the age of eleven 'from excessive dancing on his birthday'.

When Queen Anne died (her coffin was said to have been as wide as it was long) the Stock Exchange index went up by three per cent.

George II, who, according to his eldest son, was 'a miserly martinet with an insatiable sexual appetite', died of a burst blood vessel in his heart while straining on a lavatory seat.

When George II's wife Queen Caroline decided that her own children ought to be protected against smallpox with the new but highly unpredictable vaccine, she insisted on using human guinea pigs first. She had experimental inoculations performed on six condemned prisoners at Newgate prison. The men agreed to undergo the operation on condition that they would be pardoned if they survived it. Five of the prisoners recovered and walked free. The sixth kept very quiet about the fact that he'd already had smallpox and was immune, and also escaped the gallows.

When George III bought it, Buckingham Palace cost £21,000. The annual cost to Scotland Yard of protecting the Royal family today is £30 million. Costs escalated in 1982 after the Irishman Michael Fagan was allowed to wander into the Queen's bedroom unchallenged and then sit on her bed chatting to her for half an hour, and after a group of German tourists were found camping in her garden. The first unscheduled visitor to Buckingham Palace was seventeen-year-old Edward Jones, who admitted to regular break-ins between 1840–41. The boy claimed to have spent several nights in the palace and had actually sat on the throne and spent time in the royal kitchens. Jones was finally found curled up asleep under the Queen's sofa. He was rewarded for his persistence with two years on a treadmill.

In the last ten years of his reign George III spent much of his time conversing with long dead friends and indecently exposing himself to his servants. Although he was the most dramatic manifestation of 'the royal disease', almost the entire royal line of Hanover suffered from porphyria, a rare hereditary metabolic disorder with various symptoms including mental derangement. Most historians now accept that the disease has even deeper roots in the blood line of the British monarchy; it was endemic in the Stuarts, and passed to the Hanoverians by the Electress Sophia, granddaughter of James I and mother of George I.

George IV was regularly plastered on cherry brandy, which he quaffed 'in quantities not to be believed'. His appalling hangovers were legendary in London: he used to try to cure them by opening up one of his veins. Although his wishful-thinking wife spent a lot of time sticking pins into wax effigies of him and throwing them on the fire, he expired from cirrhosis of the liver.

Although George IV had one of the most corpulent backsides ever to occupy the British throne, he had the poet Leigh Hunt jailed for two years for daring to call him fat.

Caroline of Brunswick, described by a contemporary, Lady Hestor, as 'a downright whore', danced in public semi-naked, tried to seduce senior British politicians and had a string of foreign lovers. She was short, fat and ugly and, because she didn't care much for personal hygiene, stank. George IV slept with her once on their wedding night and thereafter never again: as he was blind drunk throughout and spent half the night under the grate where she left him, she was amazed when she found herself pregnant. Caroline was tried for adultery, and locked out of her own coronation at Westminster Abbey. She remained, however, far more popular than her husband.

George IV may have been a shameless spendthrift and a vain, overblown sot, but the real black sheep of the family was his younger brother Ernie. The one-eyed Duke of Cumberland was shunned by his brothers and sisters and feared by his own mother. He was suspected of having made his sister Sophia pregnant (George IV warned each of his six sisters never to be alone in the same room as Ernest) and of murdering his valet.

All of the kings of the ruling house of Hanover were noted not only for their ugliness but also for the plainness of their wives and mistresses. The attentions of George I were shared by two middle-aged ladies who, because of their somewhat contrasting figures, were known as 'The Elephant and the Maypole'. Queen Caroline of Ansbach, wife of George II, chose his mistresses for him, taking care to select only women who were even uglier than she was. George III's wife, Queen Charlotte of Mecklenburg-Stretz, was so physically repulsive it was suggested at the time that the King's bouts of madness were brought on by the trauma of having sex with her. When she arrived in England to take her throne, Londoners greeted her with cries of 'pug-face'. When Charlotte requested a translation, she was told that it meant 'God Bless Her Majesty'. George IV's mistress Maria Fitzherbert is described as having a long pointed nose and a mouth misshapen by badly fitting false teeth. He was revolted by the sight of Caroline of Brunswick, the bride his father had selected for him, the moment he clapped eyes on her. On his wedding day he went through the marriage ceremony 'looking like death', and at one point tried to run off but was restrained by his father. William IV, after proposing but being turned down by eight different women, found a bride at last in Princess Adelaide Saxe-Coburg-Meinengen, who was described by a contemporary as 'frightful'.

William IV, nicknamed 'Pineapple-Head' because of his oddly shaped dome and florid complexion, was a prolific and dedicated womaniser. In ten years he fathered ten illegitimate children by the Irish actress Dorothea Jordan alone. According to a popular story of the day, when William tried to cut back the allowance he was paying her, the actress handed him a piece of paper which at the time was attached to all playbills: it simply read: 'No money refunded after the rising of the curtain.'

When Victoria inherited Buckingham Palace in 1837 it didn't even have a bathroom. Her predecessors the Georgian royals believed it was 'sweat, damn it, that kept a man clean'.

Mealtimes with Victoria were particularly hard on her guests, especially lower-ranking visitors. Royal etiquette demanded that the Queen was always served first, and she would always start eating as soon as the food arrived. As soon as she had finished and put down her knife and fork the plate of everyone else present had to be removed immediately, thus guaranteeing that at some of her larger banquets at least half of her guests would starve. One day a brave and hungry guest insisted that the footman return his still-untouched plate to the table. Queen Victoria noticed, made enquiries about the custom and ended it.

When Victoria's son Albert carelessly shot his own brother-in-law Prince Christian in the face, Christian had to have an eye removed. He went on to collect a number of glass eyes which he was fond of producing at dinner parties and explaining the history of each at length, and became a renowned glass-eye bore. His favourite was a blood-shot one which he wore when he had a cold.

Prince Albert's father Ernest worked hard at building himself a reputation as the most enthusiastic debauchee in the dukedom of Saxe-Coburg – a position rivalled only

...nad brother Ernest Jr. The Prince ...sort, mindful that both sides of the royal family had more than a fair share of oddballs and degenerates, was genuinely worried that some of it might rub off on their son Edward. Albert subjected him to a regime of military strictness and regularly had Edward's bumps felt by a phrenologist for signs of mental instability.

Edward VII's eldest son, the Duke of Clarence, was widely suspected to have been Jack the Ripper, although he was in good company; few prominent Victorian males weren't. 'Eddie' was a regular at a notorious homosexual brothel off the Tottenham Court Road called The Hundred Guineas Club, which required members to use women's names; a strong traditionalist to the end, the Duke called himself Victoria in honour of his grandmother.

Queen Mary, who had originally been pencilled in to wed the Duke of Clarence to help hush up an affair he'd had with an Indian laundryman, but shuffled sideways to make a match with his younger brother George when the Duke died of fever, practised a legitimised form of kleptomania. She amassed a huge private collection of ornaments by willing the original owners to hand them over to her with a subtle technique which involved staring at anything that took her fancy and announcing 'I am caressing it with my eyes'. Inevitably, word got around, and her visits to stately homes were preceded by a mass panic-hiding of anything that she was likely to take a shine to. When the Queen eventually cottoned on to this, she took to turning up uninvited.

George V was an obsessive game shooter whose idea of a good time was to blaze away until he was ankle deep in spent cartridges. Even his entourage were appalled by the number of birds he killed. On one of his 'massacre shoots' at Sandringham he and six others killed 10,000 birds in four days.

George V, unlike his ancestors William II, Richard I, Edward II, Richard II, James I and William III, was vociferously homophobic. He said, 'I thought chaps like that shot themselves', and once warned, 'I won't knight buggers.'

George V was also a xenophobe, albeit a somewhat confused one, as his real surname was Saxe-Coburg-Gotha. He once proclaimed that 'abroad is awful. I know. I have been,' and wasn't coy about his dislike of foreigners, although whether in his case this meant the British isn't entirely clear.

George V's family gave his doctor permission to kill him by lethal injection, not because he was in great pain, but so that news of his death would make the morning papers.

Edward VIII, whom Hitler planned to kidnap and restore to the British throne, once boasted that 'every drop of blood in my veins is German'.

The Duke of Edinburgh, whose real surname, Schleswig-Holstein-Sonderburg-Glücksburg, was a bit too obviously Teutonic for even the royal family's liking, had three brothers-in-law who fought for Hitler, including an enthusiastic and high-ranking Nazi who was a close personal friend of Hermann Goering. None of them got an invitation to his wedding.

Princess Michael of Kent's father was a member of Hitler's SS, although, according to an official palace explanation, only an 'honorary' one.

An opinion poll taken 23 years ago showed that a third of the population of Great Britain believed that Queen Elizabeth II was chosen by God.

AD NAUSEAM

By the time Napoleon reached his Waterloo he was a complete physical wreck and may even have lost his final battle because he was in too much pain to sit on his horse. He suffered from pituitary dysplasia, which made riding difficult, and prolapsed piles and constipation, which made it well-nigh impossible. Napoleon's other complaints included syphilis, colic, a peptic ulcer and a terrible dose of cystitis (he was often observed moaning with pain every time he urinated). He also suffered from extreme fatigue, which increasingly affected his judgement and performance in battle. By Jena in 1806 his soldiers had to form a square around him while he slept through the fighting.

A survey by the American Jewish Committee in 1993 found that 38 per cent of American adults and 53 per cent of American students understood nothing by the term 'The Holocaust'.

The First Church of The Doors is the world's most marginal religious cult. They worship Jim Morrison (lead singer of The Doors until he died, a bloated heroin addict, in his bath) as a god. In 1990 two members of the cult were caught attempting to rob his grave.

Mary Mallon – 'Typhoid Mary' to her friends – was the most notorious disease carrier ever. In her job as a New York cook between 1906 and 1915, she made a huge personal contribution to the 1903 typhoid epidemic. Fifty-three outbreaks of typhoid, including three deaths, were directly attributed to her. Mary Mallon spent the last 23 years of life under permanent hospital detention.

In North America one million trees are cut down every year to be used for junk mail.

Doctors were baffled for years by the rarest of diseases, Kuru, which only ever occurred among the Fore tribe of Papua New Guinea. The virus was apparently transmitted during ritual mourning when the brains of the dead were handled by women and children. Kuru had another more popular name: 'laughing sickness'.

Seventy-five million children worldwide under the age of fifteen are forced to work for a living.

Ludwig van Beethoven, Franz Schubert, Paganini, Robert Schumann, Frederick Delius, Albrecht Dürer, Rembrandt, Francisco Goya, Edouard Manet, Henri Toulouse-Lautrec, Paul Gauguin, John Milton, Jonathan Swift, John Keats and Oscar Wilde were all syphilitic.

According to his dad, the young Charles Darwin was only ever interested in shooting dogs and rat-catching.

During World War I, one in three British servicemen suffered from venereal disease – a much higher percentage than other European nations, largely because the British soldier alone was completely denied counselling on the avoidance or treatment of the disease. Not that too many soldiers minded: as VD was usually a passport away from front-line service, many tried to catch it deliberately. Back in England, prostitutes found they could charge Tommies extra because they offered the hope of invaliding them out of service. Some soldiers were caught selling venereal discharge to their comrades, while others deliberately infected their eyes, unwittingly risking permanent blindness.

The Black Death, which wiped out a quarter of the population of Europe, may have been the result of the first-ever recorded episode of biological warfare. The origin of the epidemic in Europe has been traced to the trading post at Caffa on the Russian shore of the Black Sea. Infected Tartars from the east besieged a group of Genoese merchants who were holed up in the trading post, and used catapults to throw the corpses of their own infected dead over the wall. When the siege was over the Genoese took the disease home to Italy with them.

The worldwide annual expenditure on arms is approximately £3 trillion.

Happiness is . . .

According to some leading psychologists, happiness may be a form of insanity. Miserable people tend to have a far more realistic and objective view of life: if you think that people are talking about you behind your back it's because they really are.

The most popular time to commit suicide is on a Monday or Tuesday afternoon in the spring.

Hans Klaus from Kiel, West Germany is the world's most unsuccessful suicide. He failed in 28 attempts on his own life, including ten slashed wrists, four poisonings, two hangings, stabbing, gassing, drowning and drug overdosing. He finally gave up after throwing himself out of a fourth floor window and landing on a passer-by.

In the USA someone is attempting suicide every minute of the day.

The most common methods of suicide are hanging or suffocation for males, and poisoning for females.

For each successful suicide, there are fifteen failed attempts.

The most miserly person who ever lived was an American woman, Henrietta Howland Green. Although the total extent of her wealth was never revealed, she was known to have kept a balance of nearly $31.5 million in one bank alone. Her son had to have his leg amputated because she spent too long searching for a free clinic, and she ate cold porridge because she was too mean to heat it. She lived mostly on onion and eggs, and wore old newspaper when her petticoats wore out. She died aged 81 in 1916, leaving an estate worth $95 million.

The affluent 18th-century farm-owner Daniel Dancer, of Harrow Weald was believed to be the most miserly Briton of his time. Although he inherited a fortune he even heated his food by sitting on it.

Martin Luther suffered from chronic constipation.

Every year, one million unwanted pets are put down in Britain.

It wasn't the bravery of Cortez's Spanish *conquistadores* that subdued the once mighty Mexico, but the smallpox he brought with him. The Incas had no opportunity to build up resistance to European infections, and Cortez learned quickly that the locals were highly vulnerable to a disease against which his own soldiers had considerable immunity. He even helped spread the disease by handing out infected blankets to the Incas. Before Cortez the total population of Mexico was 25 to 30 million. Within 50 years it was 2.3 to 3 million, and within another 50 years it had halved again.

Every year two million battery hens die prematurely because of the conditions they live in.

The town of Waterloo in Belgium has a tomb for an English soldier's leg.

Although Columbus has been blamed for bringing syphilis to Europe (the first recorded incidence was 1496, four years after he landed in the West Indies), the disease has been around since prehistoric times. A syphilitic bone dating from 2,500 BC has been found in the Gobi desert, and in the fourth century Hippocrates described a syphilitic-like disease whose symptoms included 'rotting of the genitals'. When it first appeared in Europe it was a much more deadly disease than it is today, and it rapidly swept through the continent on a terrifying scale. The French armies of Charles VIII, ravaging Italy and its women, picked it up from Genoese sailors via prostitutes and carried it home to France. It spread to Britain, Germany and Holland, then east as far as China. It was originally known as 'French Sickness'.

In October 1992 an Australian judge awarded £32,000 damages to a man who had cut off his own penis.

A single sneeze can distribute 80 million bacteria at a distance of 12 feet. The bacteria remains suspended in the air for 30 minutes. The influenza epidemic which started shortly before the end of World War I killed twice as many people in a few months than both sides had managed in four years of fighting. The origin of the virus was unknown, but in a matter of weeks it had spread to five continents. It was variously known as Spanish flu (England), Bolshevik disease (Poland), Black Whip (Hungary), Flanders grippe (among British servicemen), Wind Disease (Persia), Cold Disease (India), the Great Cold Fever (Thailand), Wrestler's Fever (Japan) and Blitz Catarrh (Germany).

The Russo-Japanese war of 1904–1906 was a landmark in major military encounters because it was the first war ever fought in which the number of combatants killed by enemy action exceeded the number of men killed by disease.

Dentists in England and Wales extract about four tonnes of rotten teeth from children each year.

In the USA 250 million wild animals are killed by people on hunting holidays every year.

When the US government exploded nuclear test bombs in the Nevada desert in the 1950s, many people living about 40 miles away in Las Vegas complained that the A-bomb blasts weren't spectacular enough. Residents living downwind of the fallout meanwhile were offered a free car wash if their vehicles had picked up radioactive dust. The small town of St George, 135 miles away was found to have received radiation doses about 3,500 times greater than the maximum permitted level considered safe for nuclear workers at that time.

Ruminating animals release about 80 million tons of methane into the atmosphere every year.

Before Robert Louis Stevenson took up drugs and fornication as his favourite forms of relaxation – he was so highly sexed that he helped keep most of Edinburgh's prostitutes in business – he had a strict Calvinist upbringing which made him so pious that he would try to convert sheep by reading aloud to them passages from the Bible.